STRATEGIC DECISIONS FOR SMALL BUSINESS

STRATEGIC DECISIONS FOR SMALL BUSINESS

It's Just Noodles,
This Ain't No Trattoria

R. BLAKE HENDRIX

iUniverse, Inc.
New York Lincoln Shanghai

Strategic Decisions for Small Business
It's Just Noodles, This Ain't No Trattoria

iUniverse books may be ordered through booksellers or by contacting:

iUniverse
2021 Pine Lake Road, Suite 100
Lincoln, NE 68512
www.iuniverse.com
1-800-Authors (1-800-288-4677)

The information, ideas, and suggestions in this book are not intended to render professional advice. Before following any suggestions contained in this book, you should consult your personal accountant or other financial advisor. Neither the author nor the publisher shall be liable or responsible for any loss or damage allegedly arising as a consequence of your use or application of any information or suggestions in this book.

ISBN-13: 978-0-595-42314-9 (pbk)
ISBN-13: 978-0-595-86652-6 (ebk)
ISBN-10: 0-595-42314-0 (pbk)
ISBN-10: 0-595-86652-2 (ebk)

Printed in the United States of America

DEDICATION AND SPECIAL THANKS

This book is dedicated to my lovely wife Laura and her son, my stepson, Tyler. They have been both supportive and understanding in my work. I offer special thanks to Matt Huculak, at the University of Tulsa. He was invaluable for his assistance in citation and editing. Finally, I recognize Sean H. and Tom A. for changing the trajectory of my life. I thank you all.

CONTENTS

Part II

Practice

INTRODUCTION

It's Just Noodles, This Ain't No Trattoria

Nearly twenty years ago, I arrived in New Orleans to earn a Master of Business Administration degree at Tulane. New Orleans was a real "step-up" in the world for me since I was raised in a small Arkansas town. As an undergraduate, I enrolled at the University of Arkansas to earn a degree in economics; at the time, Fayetteville, Arkansas seemed like a metropolis. The first place I lived in New Orleans was in the Garden District, a block or so off Magazine Street. I rented a small, furnished efficiency apartment that was part of an historic, camel back, brick, double, row house. The owner, Daniel, occupied one-half of the lower floors with a tenant in the adjoining space and me in the hump.

As I recall, the home was built in the 1840's by a General whose name I've forgotten. It seems as if the name was Beau-something-or-another and was at Camp and 3rd. It was a registered historic home and a beautiful show-place. My apartment was small but nicely furnished, and I struck a friend-ship with Daniel over time that I have very much enjoyed. He had retired from the film industry and split his time between Paris and New Orleans.

On my second night in New Orleans, Daniel invited me to dinner at a comfortable, neighborhood restaurant just a couple of blocks from our home that served Creole fare and specialized in fish. Over drinks, Daniel told me all about New Orleans: Where to go, what to stay away from, local custom, Mardi gras. He also told how to get out of jail if I ran across some unfortunate situation—advice that I used during my first Mardi gras. He was a regular at the restaurant and asked the waiter to bring us "the usual." The usual was a small salad, a small pasta course followed by

Redfish. He treated me to a wonderful French wine I'd never heard of and we had a grand time. When the pasta course was served, I had a puzzled look on my face. The source of bewilderment was a combination of being overwhelmed by New Orleans and not understanding why my plate of pasta was so small. At that point Daniel looked at me and said, "it's just noodles, this ain't no trattoria." I smiled and we continued our meal and conversation. I took Daniel to mean the following: You aren't in a fancy restaurant, certainly by New Orleans standards. You have food in front of you and a glass of wine. Enjoy it! The memory of that meal has remained over the years and I've taken his phrase to heart.

This is the theme of the book; keeping things in perspective as you map and achieve your business goals. This book targets the small businessperson. I draw upon my academic training and over 15 years business experience as an accountant, commercial banker and consultant in serving this market. I surveyed the daunting number of books on business strategy and found many books that were quite informative. What I *did not* find was a discussion of strategic decisions stressing *simplicity and perspective* adequately for the small businessperson. Much of the research and discussion of strategic planning is geared toward the Fortune 500 (the largest corporations in America). The desire is to take the best information offered by the body of research and practice, boil it down and apply it to the small business. The principles are the same for the Fortune 500 and the small business; *it is only a matter of adjusting the frame.* I draw upon the basics of economics, game theory, strategic thinking and experience to show you how to integrate strategy, logistics and tactics in mapping and achieving your business goals. I coin this integration the "SaLT" Method.

In this book you will not find great depth; rather, you will find breadth and perspective written in an amusing, informative manner. This text compiles *relevant* economic, strategic and game theory principles and explains them in a useful and understandable format for the small businessperson. Supply and demand, diminishing returns, oligopoly theory, game theory and strategic models are covered in an *approachable* fashion for application. The universe of theory has not been covered, *as all encompassing* knowledge is not required. The relevant information is sufficiently surveyed to offer *practical* advice and application in decision making. Theoretical knowledge is coupled with experience and insight to offer steps used in finding solutions to problems facing the small businessperson. This is the essence of the SaLT Method.

I like to call this book "that vision thing." It is specifically designed not only the give you the perspective of the big picture, but also a framework to determine who you are, who you want to be and how to get there.

Two other ideas that I have for future topics include financial statement analysis and financing alternatives for the small businessperson. Again there are a number of texts on these two subjects, but I think a different approach would better serve you, the small businessperson. Those texts tend to become bogged down in detail and miss the main point: You are trying to run a business. You don't need to be an expert of theory; however, an understanding of simple concepts can at least signal to you that you need to wear a life preserver as you step into deep water. A saying from where I grew up dates back to the turn of the 20th century. It goes, "it's a considerate husband who leaves his wife with a sharp ax." Let's define your vision and give you a sharp tool to make strategic choices.

RBH
Tulsa, Oklahoma
May 11, 2006

PART I

Theory

This book is divided into two parts: The first is theory and the second is practice. In Part I, I will cover basic economic and game theory using often inane examples to illustrate my point. In terms of sources, I have relied heavily on the Internet and have kept in mind the *Chicago Manual of Style's*[1] comments on electronic sources, which stress paying careful attention to the concepts of permanence and authority. In my experience, I find the Internet valuable for its scope and accessibility. However, one must be especially attentive to authority. For example, a popular work may easily be found online without citation. It may misrepresent the author or not attribute a source at all. Where possible and meaningful, I have avoided sources on the Internet where the original source can't be located. Notwithstanding the risks inherent in the Internet, it does offer readers the ability to find a source document on their own allowing them to read the entire work if they wish. In addition, many of the works cited in this text are obscure and the Internet allows convenient reference not otherwise available. Chapters are organized topically for ease of reference and reading. Chapter organization, combined with the index and notes, allows the reader access to all relevant concepts.

CHAPTER 1

That Vision Thing

Ronald Reagan was able to mobilize and inspire his followers because he was skilled at presenting his vision to the public. In contrast, George H. W. Bush admitted he wasn't big on "that vision thing." George H.W. Bush couldn't communicate his vision for America's Economy, America's Foreign Policy and a New World Order. His seeming lack of vision contributed to his loss in the 1992 presidential election.

It has been over twenty-five years since Reagan took office and certain images are still conjured by his Presidency. Remember, I am addressing vision as it is *perceived*. I am not judging or validating a legacy other than the articulated vision. Political scientists and historians are charged with judgments as to policy and its success or not. You can control your vision, and to an extent, how it is perceived. A well-articulated vision, especially if it is *apropos*, will allow you to forge ahead in reaching your goals.

When I remember the Reagan Presidency, two things pop into my head:

1. It's Morning in America
2. Shining City on a Hill

Underlying this vision is the notion of hope and return to the "right" path. Some quip too "right" but the vision is clear. Post-Nixon America was wrestling with distrust of its leaders, a hangover from Vietnam, (or as some would say, recovery from the Asian flu) gasoline lines, and a combination of inflation and low growth, coined "stagflation." Central to Reagan's vision was Reaganomics, which embraced the free market and declared, "government isn't the solution to our problems; government is the problem."[2] The emotive campaign ad proclaiming "It's morning again in

---

3

America" in the 1984 presidential campaign was a marketing *coup* in articulating Reagan's vision. Reagan's constant invocation of the "shining city on the hill," and "you ain't seen nothing yet," marked his approach.[3] Early in his presidency, Reagan remarked, "What I'd really like to do is go down in history as the President who made Americans believe in themselves again."[4]

Fair or not; substantive or not, George H.W. Bush evokes three images:

1. The Checkout Scanner Debacle
2. Read My Lips
3. That Vision thing

Bush's supposed confusion as to the nature and purpose of a checkout scanner while buying a pair of socks in the 1992-election cycle was startling. "Read my lips, no new taxes" was a strong promise that Bush was unable to keep. In the 1992 campaign, these images, coupled with his referral to "that vision thing," all paint a portrait of a Presidency out of touch with the people. It leaves the impression of a President without a clear vision for the nation. You need a clear vision for your business, just as a President needs a clear vision for the nation.

Adam Smith, considered by many as the father of "classical"[5] economics, characterized the entrepreneur as the "butcher, the brewer or the baker." In his familiar quote in the chapter describing the motivation of labor he says, "It is not from the benevolence of the butcher, the brewer or the baker, that we expect our dinner, but from their regard to their own interest." The entrepreneur does not perform his task to benefit his customer, but to benefit his own table. Smith continues, "We address ourselves, not to their humanity but to their self-love, and never talk to them of our own necessities but of their advantages."[6] In my business career, first in accounting, then in finance, I have evaluated scores of businesses and helped countless business owners prepare financial statements, evaluate business plans, borrow money, gauge risk, solve problems and celebrate successes. These businesses are generally smaller in size and are run by the founder of the company. In business service terms, they are labeled as small business customers; they are the entrepreneur class of our economy.

These entrepreneurs share many of the same characteristics. Without fail, they are:

Ambitious	Hard-working
Brave	Innovative
Creative	Persistent
Dedicated	Passionate
Determined	Risk-taking
Efficient	Resilient

Certainly some characteristics have been omitted. But the small businessperson has a distinctive flavor captured by the words above. You are also overworked, at times overwhelmed and generally under-capitalized. You may be a market leader in your town or hamlet with several generations of family working in the business. Revenue size and the number of employees can vary widely, but at a minimum, the smallest entrepreneur has at least 10 employees even if the entrepreneur is a one-person shop. The entrepreneur functions in many roles:

Accountant/Bookkeeper
Accounts Receivable Specialist
Inventory Specialist
Administrative Specialist
Human Resources Director
Finance Director
Sales Director
Marketing Director
President
Chairman of the Board

The company may provide professional services, such as doctors, lawyers and accountants do. The company may sell retail or wholesale goods. It could be a distributor. The company may manufacture the widget or be in construction. The goods or services could be marketed from a storefront, plant or over the Internet.

Whatever the nature of the business, it exists to provide food for the founder's table and feed his family. The founder may have ambitions to become a global juggernaut one-day, see the company's stock in the Dow Jones Industrial Average, become part of the Fortune 500, become a franchiser or simply provide a business for his kids to one day manage. This sounds very similar to the butcher, baker or brewer that Adam Smith described.

Smith lived from 1723 to 1790. Born in Scotland, his academic studies were in European Literature at Balloil College at Oxford. In 1764, he became tutor to the Duke of Buccleuch and traveled on the Continent for two years. Having earned a life pension from tutoring the Duke, he retired to Scotland to write *The Wealth of Nations (1776)*. Smith has garnered a reputation as being ruthless or selfish, but in his writing *The Theory of Moral Sentiments (1759)*, he argued that the nature of man possessed principles that caused him to want to see his fellow man prosper if for no other reason than it pleased his nature.[7]

As the founder's business grows in size over time, generalizations can be made about the corporate culture of the organization. Over time the founder's stamp may be incorporated in the culture which can eventually become distinct from that of the founder. Graphically, the transition from founder's culture to corporate culture can be depicted as follows (management's personality is also included in the representation):

Graph 1.1—Influence

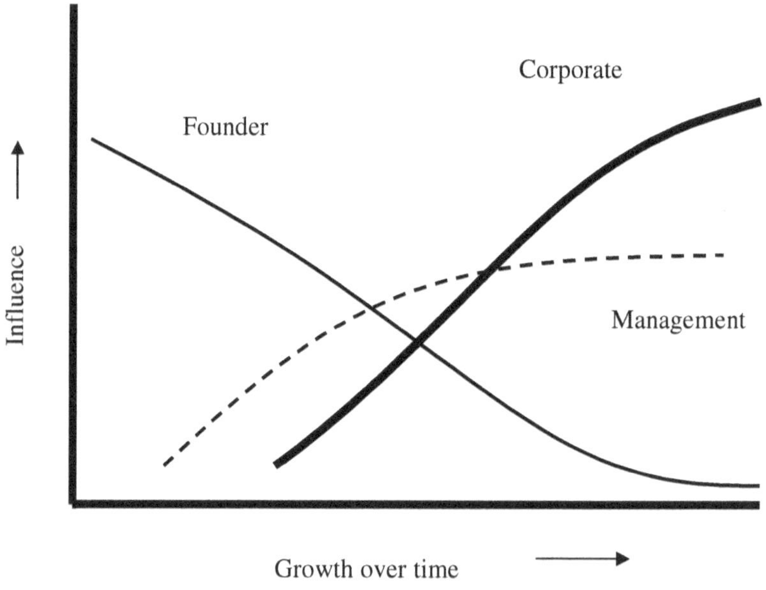

The graph reiterates the obvious; over time, the founder's influence will wane. It does not attempt to plot the timing of the transition points as the founder's influence declines and corporate culture becomes more dominant. The transition point will be unique to every organization. It is doubtful an algorithm could predict this exact point. What is more important is the integration itself. Pascal Levensohn wrote a paper documenting the need for founder transition along with warning signs. He also makes the point that the company's transition away from the founder is a "natural evolution"[8] as the company grows. He lists six warning signs[9] for the need of transition:

1. Staying the wrong course
2. Out of touch
3. Emotional and combative behavior
4. Withholding information from management
5. Directing management to withhold information
6. Blaming others

The founder's personality influences and is influenced by the corporate culture and management's personality. The interaction can be viewed in Graph 1.2.

Graph 1.2—Founder, management personality → Corporate Culture

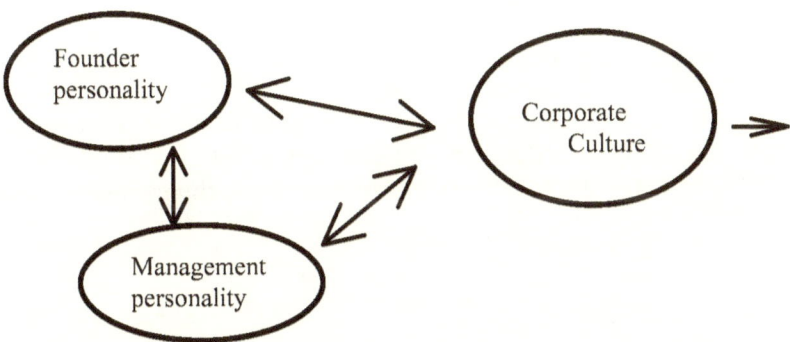

This integration of personalities into corporate culture ultimately becomes what I term the integration of strategy, logistics and tactics, or SaLT of the company. Through the lens of SaLT, the company navigates its way to the future. SaLT is vitally important in achieving its goals.

Graph 1.3 illustrates the interaction of SaLT with the intended path of the business. As we will see in later chapters, the lens of SaLT is not always integrated, nor may it describe the intended path. Graph 1.3, pictures an ideal integration of plan with intended outcome.

Graph 1.3—SaLT

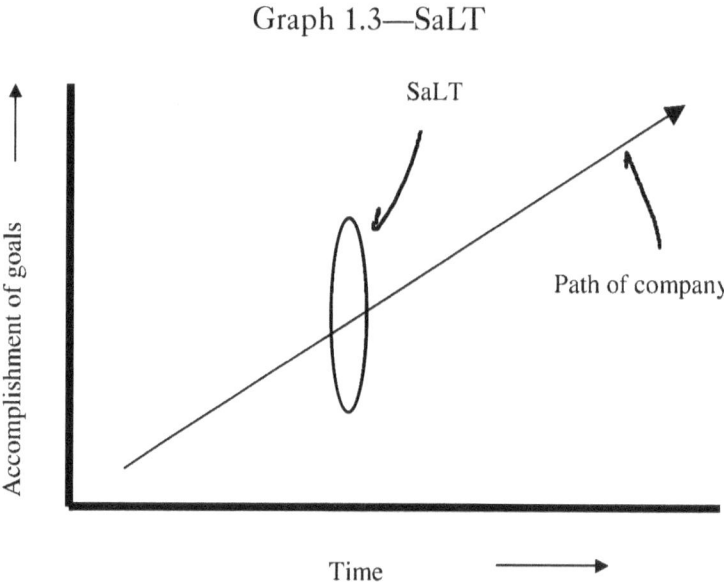

SaLT Concept

SaLT is the integration of strategy, logistics and tactics to accomplish your objective. I will further develop the concept of SaLT throughout this book, ultimately developing a methodology to apply the concept.

CHAPTER 2

Guns and Butter

"But we will not permit those who fire upon us in Vietnam to win victory over the desires and the intentions of all the American People. This Nation is mighty enough, its society is healthy enough, its people are strong enough, to pursue our goals in the rest of the world while still building a Great Society here at home."

—Lyndon B. Johnson. January 12, 1966[10]

Lyndon Johnson believed he could have guns *and* butter. Guns and butter are the classic example of the economist's production possibilities curve. The "Production Possibilities Curve" graphically illustrates the tradeoff an economic system faces in producing two commodities—guns and butter in this case. Johnson felt America was strong enough and wealthy enough to provide for both his Great Society programs at home and for the war in Vietnam. The day after his speech the *Washington Post* ran the following headline according to Robert Dallek:

"U.S. Can Continue the 'Great Society' and Fight in Vietnam …
—LBJ Hands Congress Massive Work Load."[11]

Dallek summarizes Johnson's ambitions as unrealistic saying, "… his whole economic plan for fighting the war and advancing the Great Society, were illusions that the realities of 1966 would largely dispell [sic]."[12]

There are camps of thought that would blame the firing of inflation, which crested in the late 1970's, as a direct result of Johnson's policies.

David Ricardo was born in England in 1772 and was heavily influenced by Smith's writings. He acquired a fortune on the London Stock Exchange and retired to academics. In his work published in 1817, *On Principles of Political Economy and Taxation*, he concluded that trade between countries was influenced by relative costs and price structures resulting in the comparative advantage of one trading partner over another for a class of goods.[13]

Ricardo postulated that if Portugal could produce wine with 80 men per year and cloth with the labor of 90, she should employ her resources in the production of wine. If in England it required 100 men to produce cloth, it was still to Portugal's advantage to employ capital in wine even though it took fewer men than England to produce cloth. She could acquire more cloth by trading wine than utilizing her own resources to produce cloth.[14] This analysis led to modern depiction of the Production Possibilities Curve. Ricardo died at age 51 in 1823.

Graph 2.1—Production Possibilities Curve (PPC)—Guns and Butter

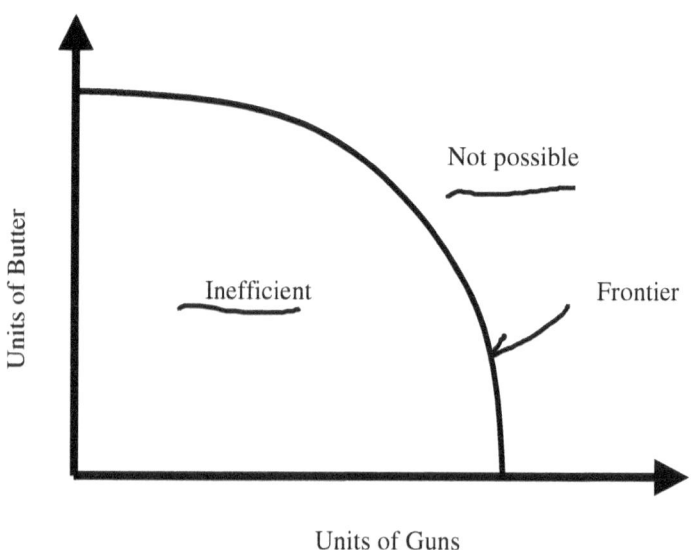

The PPC shows the maximum output of guns and butter or combination thereof that an economy can produce. It is constrained by the availability of resources, technology and management expertise. Production to the

right of the curve is not possible. Production inside the curve is inefficient, since more of both commodities can be produced. The curved line is the efficient frontier of production possible. There are obviously more than two commodities in an economy. The analysis is performed for only two commodities so the model can be simplified and conclusions can be drawn. This is discussed further in the chapter *Ceteris Paribus*.

The curve is derived by theoretically summing all the production of firms in an economy. Imagine three firms in our economy: A, B and C. The production capabilities of these firms can be graphed as follows:

Graph 2.2—PPC firms A, B and C

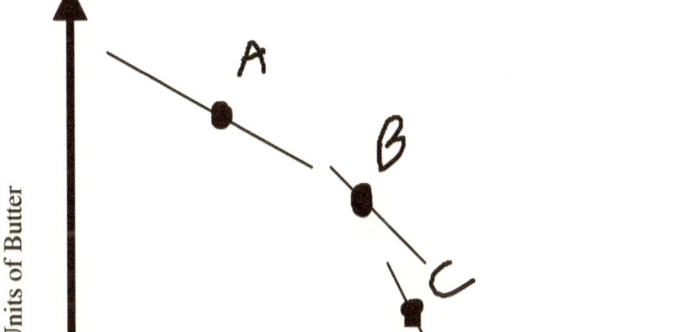

Firm A has a production function depicted by the line labeled A. B and C have similar functions with differing combinations of guns and butter.

When we combine all the common production points of all the firms in the economy we are left with the PPC.

Graph 2.3—Combined PPC for the economy

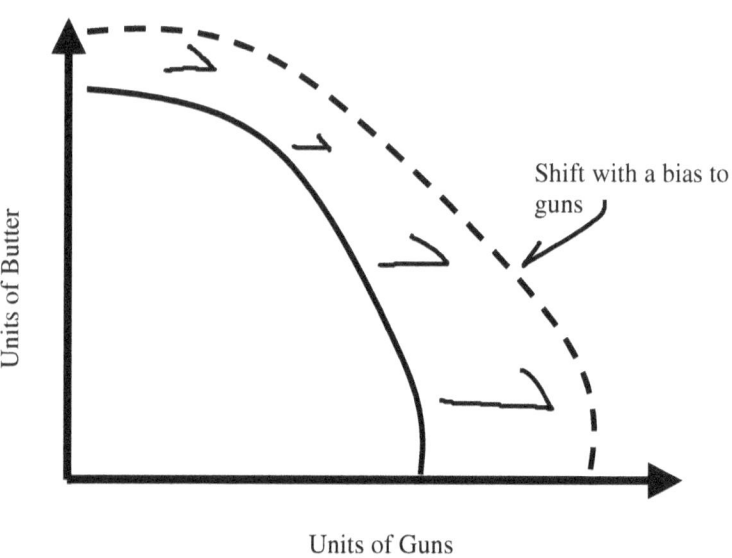

Units of Butter

Shift with a bias to guns

Units of Guns

Shifts in the curve can occur if production technologies are improved for guns or butter, or both. Outward shifts occur when production technologies for both products improve. There also exists a bias to guns when technology for the production of guns improves versus that of butter. Conversely, there is a bias to butter when technology for the production of butter relatively improves.

For our purposes, the most important concept is that of opportunity cost. In simple terms, opportunity cost is what you give up to get something else. In the context of the PPC, it is slope of any point on the frontier. This is known as the marginal rate of transformation and is derived from the Principle of Scarcity.

Graph 2.4—PPC, Opportunity Costs

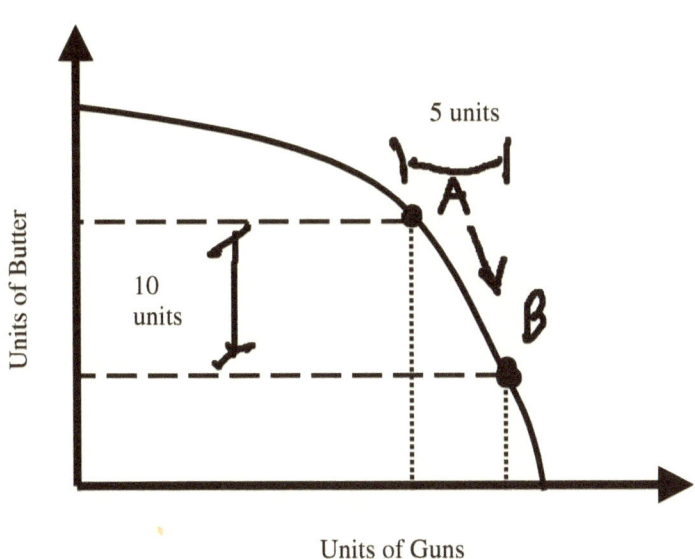

Units of Guns

Because resources are limited and scarce, to move from point A to point B you may give up 10 units of butter to gain 5 units of guns. The marginal rate of transformation of butter for guns is 2 units. You must give up 2 units of butter for every gun unit gained.

In 1932, Lionel Robbins penned his famous work, *An Essay on the Nature and Significance of Economic Science.* In the book he defines economics as, "that science that studies the relationship between ends and means that have alternative uses."[15] Robbins' definition of economics encompasses both concepts of scarcity and opportunity costs. The wants and needs of humanity exceed the resources available. Because goods are scarce, resources have opportunity costs that are inherent in their allocation.

Our analysis of Production Possibilities need not be limited to guns or butter. You can substitute any two items and reach the same concept of opportunity cost. Try steel and broccoli in the analysis; pigs and cars; corn and Bourbon. They all fit into the framework.

SaLT Concept

Resources are limited. Goods have "value" or "cost" in the framework of allocation of those resources to produce one good over another. As we shall see, opportunity costs apply to the consumption of goods as well.

CHAPTER 3

Law of Diminishing Returns

Thomas Robert Malthus lived from 1766 to 1834 and was consumed with the notion that population growth would exceed the food supply. He felt this way since the amount of arable land available for farming was fixed. This Malthusian Catastrophe did not recognize technological advances in farming, such as differing seed strains, pesticides and fertilizers, *et cetera*. Malthus studied philosophy and mathematics at Jesus College in Cambridge[16] and was an ordained minister.[17] According to Malthus, "All the checks to population … are clearly resolvable into moral restraint, vice and misery."[18] Malthus felt it one's duty to "restrain our passions."[19]

The Law of Diminishing Returns is summarized as such:

When one of the factors of production is fixed, increasing the other factors will lead to an increase in returns up to a point. Beyond this point, returns will diminish. The classic model varies the amount of labor available; however, the conclusions also hold true for the demand curve or consumption curve.

A Classic Version

Imagine a farm growing wheat. There are a number of jobs that need to be accomplished at harvest time and they must be done in a short period of time. The wheat must be cut and gathered, the chaff separated. The harvested crop must be taken to a silo, weighed, dried and stored. The machinery needs to be maintained, paperwork completed and breakfast, lunch and dinner prepared for the hands. One man working alone will not be able to complete all of these tasks. By dividing labor there will be gains in productivity as labor is added. Productivity will be enhanced by specialization and time not wasted by switching between tasks.

Table 3.1—Hypothetical Workers and Bushels of Wheat

Workers	TPP	MPP
0	0	N/A
1	100	100
2	300	200
3	900	600
4	1,200	300
5	1,300	100
6	1,200	<200>

The amount of land, seed, fertilizer and water employed is fixed. TPP and MPP are defined as follows:

Total Physical Product equals total bushels of wheat produced. Marginal Physical Product is the change in output as input changes.

Graph 3.1—TPP

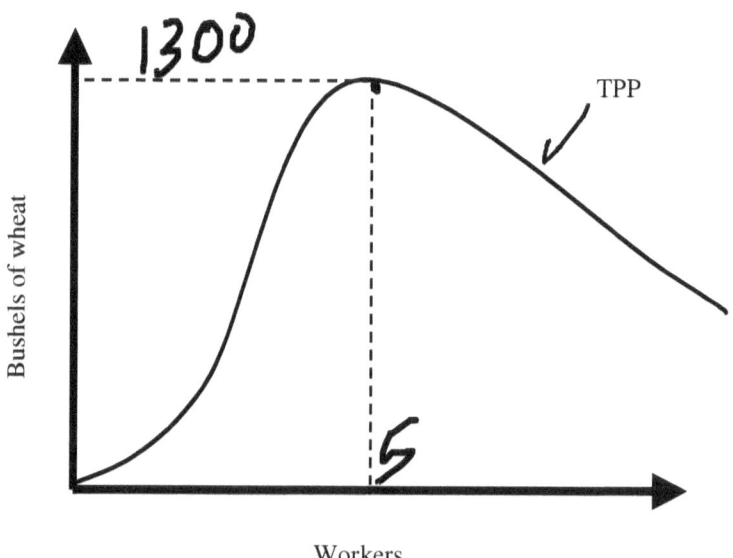

Given our production function, output of wheat will be maximized at 1,300 bushels while employing five workers. Marginal Physical Product for our production of wheat is graphically displayed below.

Graph 3.2—MPP of Wheat

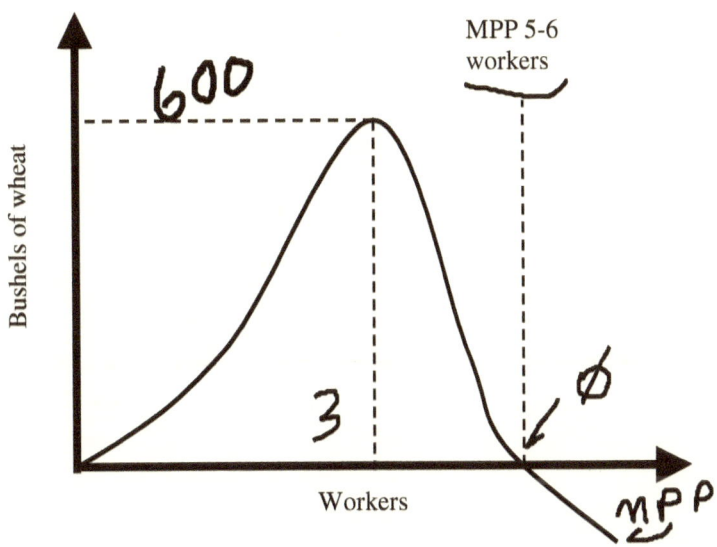

MPP peaks at three workers, and produces 600 bushels for the 3rd worker. MPP is zero between 5 and 6 workers causing output to fall on an absolute basis. The point at three workers is the point of diminishing returns. Additional labor adds to production, but at a lower rate than before. Let's consider TPP and MPP on an intuitive basis. If we employed no workers, output would obviously be zero. Assuming on our acre of land we employed an infinite number of workers, output would also be zero as the workers would trample the crop. As we add workers, production rises only to a point. Beyond that point additional workers are detrimental to production. Workers at some point are too much of a good thing! This analysis can be performed for any inputs of production. Let's take it a step further. Let's show the relationship between money and happiness. In economic terms we would graph money earned versus the utility of money.

Graph 3.3—MPP of Money Earned

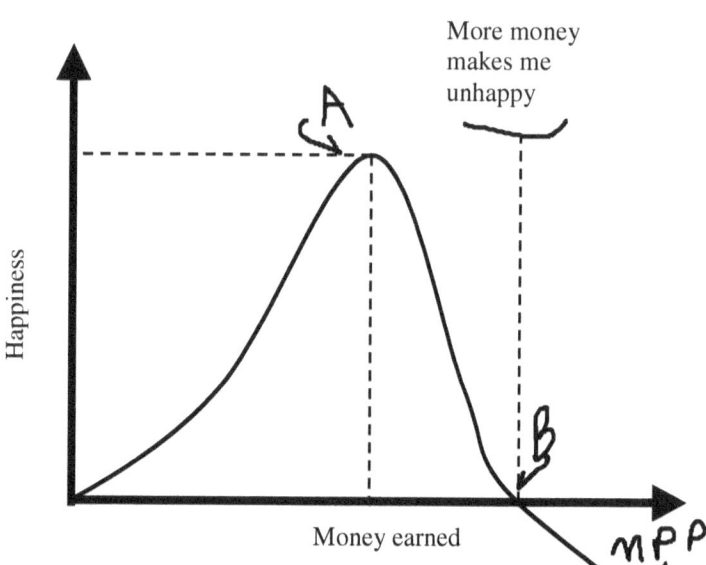

This graph shows the Marginal Physical Product (or marginal utility) of money earned through labor. Happiness is the utility function for money. More money, more happiness, right? As money earned increases, happiness does too, first at a fast rate, but then a slower rate as diminishing returns set in (point A). At some point, earning more money would begin to make you unhappy. At point A, the last dollar earned made you happiest relative to the other dollars. Between point A & B, money still adds to happiness but at a slower rate. Beyond point B, more money actually makes you less happy. This makes sense empirically, as well as intuitively. Think of your college days when finding a quarter under the seat cushion was occasion for a party. With that quarter you could buy a glass of beer at happy hour. Now think of Bill Gates seeing a $100 bill lying on the street. Would he stoop to pick it up? At what point do you hire to have your lawn cut? The point that you would pay not to perform the labor yourself.

SaLT Concepts

There are four conclusions and implications of the Law of Diminishing Returns for the purposes of this book:

1. Just like production, money and happiness are relative things, which are related—at least in part—to how much money you have.

2. Over the life of an asset, inputs will provide less and less profit at the margin.

3. Over the life of a product, the product will provide less and less profit at the margin.

4. Over the life of a business, reinvested profit will provide less and less additional profit over time.

CHAPTER 4

Money Versus Values

According to *Encyclopedia Britannica*, money is "a commodity accepted by general consent as a medium of economic exchange. It is the medium in which prices and values are expressed; as currency, it circulates anonymously from person to person and country to country, thus facilitating trade, and it is the principal measure of wealth." We are used to money being expressed as dollars, yen or pesos, but this has not always been the case. Anything can serve as money if it is generally accepted. Beads, whale's teeth, shells, tobacco, cigarettes, stones and cattle have all been a medium of exchange (to mention just a few).[20]

In Milton Friedman's book, *Money Mischief*, he discusses the humorous story of the stone money of the island of Yap in the Pacific. In 1903, William Henry Furness III spent several months on the island doing anthropological studies. In his book, *The Island of Stone Money*, he describes the monetary system of Uap (Yap):

> ... As their island yields no metal, they have had recourse to stone, on which labour in fetching and fashioning has been expended, is truly a representation of labour as the mined and minted coins of civilisation.
>
> Their medium of exchange they call *fei*, and it consists of large, solid, thick, stone wheels, ranging in diameter from a foot to twelve feet, having in the center a hole varying in size with the diameter of the stone, wherein a pole may be inserted sufficiently large and strong to bear the weight and facilitate transportation. These stone "coins" [which were made from limestone found on an island some four hundred miles distant. They] were originally quarried and

shaped [on that island and the product] brought to Uap by some venturesome native navigators, in canoes and on rafts....

A noteworthy feature of the stone currency ... is that it is not necessary for its owner to reduce it to a possession. After conducting a bargain which involves the price of a *fei* too large to be conveniently moved, its new owner is quite content to accept the bare acknowledgment of ownership and without so much as a mark to indicate the exchange, the coin remains undisturbed on the former owner's premises.

My faithful old friend, Fatumak, assured me that there was [in the] village near-by a family whose wealth was unquestioned—acknowledged by everyone—and yet no one, not even the family itself, had ever laid eye or hand on this wealth; it consisted of an enormous *fei*, whereof the size is known only by tradition; for the past two or three generations it had been, and at that very time was lying at the bottom of the sea! Many years ago an ancestor of this family, on an expedition after *fei*, secured this remarkably large and exceeding valuable stone, which was placed on a raft to be towed homeward. A violent storm arose, and the party to save their lives, were obliged to cut the raft adrift and the stone sank out of sight. When they reached home, they all testified that the *fei* was of magnificent proportions and of extraordinary quality, and that it was lost through no fault of the owner. Thereupon it was universally conceded in their simple faith that the mere accident of its loss overboard was too trifling to mention, and that a few hundred feet of water off shore ought not to affect its marketable value, since it was all chipped out in proper form. The purchasing power of that stone remains, therefore, as valid as if it were leaning visibly against the side of the owner's house....

Fei are not prized merely because they are old, nor have they sanctity as the legendary work of gods or ancient heroes. This was proved by an enterprising Irish-American copra trader, who, while living in Uap, carried on for many years a brisk, profitable trade by sending a schooner to [an island where *fei* were quarried] with several natives, experts all in the essentials of *fei*. There the stones were quarried, properly shaped, and the schooner returned with a full cargo of genuine wealth, which was given in exchange for tons of dried coconut.... [21]

Friedman points out how important belief and acceptance are in monetary matters. Our own monetary system seems completely rational while the yen and peso may seem to some as irrational as stones or beads.[22]

Most economic analysis centers on price as a measurement of value. However, price (or money) is not the only form of value. Economists move away from this a bit by speaking of the "Utility Function" that measures value or happiness. Price and money are shorthand for utility.

Value should not be confused with values. *The Oxford American Dictionary* defines values as "one's principles or standards; one's judgment of what is valuable or important in life." *One of the cornerstones of SaLT is understanding your own values, or what is important to you in life.* An understanding of one's own values is critical in the determination of what goal one is trying to accomplish.

According to Stanton Peele, a psychologist who has written on values and addiction, "Your values are your beliefs that some things are right and good and others wrong or bad, that some things are more important that others, and that one way of doing things is better than another. Values are usually deeply held—They come from your earliest learning and back-ground. Values reflect what your parents taught you, what you learned in school and religious institutions, and what the social and cultural groups you belong to hold to be true and right."[23]

Peele's Core Values:[24]

1. Achievement—in work or providing for your family
2. Consciousness—being awake, alert and aware
3. Activity—energetic and engaged
4. Health—in mind and body
5. Responsibility—fulfilling commitments
6. Self-respect—caring for yourself and others
7. Community—contributing to the welfare of the world

Peele maps these general values as objectives to strive for. Fulfilling these values will help you become balanced, perceptive and fulfilled.

SaLT Concept

Money is not the only measure or form of value. Understanding your core values, whatever they may be, are central to applying SaLT.

CHAPTER 5

Ceteris Paribus

A mathematician, an accountant and an economist apply for the same job.

The interviewer calls in the mathematician and asks "What do two plus two equal?" The mathematician replies "Four." The interviewer asks "Four, exactly?" The mathematician looks at the interviewer incredulously and says "Yes, four, exactly."

Then the interviewer calls in the accountant and asks the same question. "What do two plus two equal?" The accountant says "On average, four—give or take ten percent, but on average, four."

Then the interviewer calls in the economist and poses the same question "What do two plus two equal?" The economist gets up, locks the door, closes the shade, sits down next to the interviewer and says, "What do you want it to equal?"

—Joke circulating in e-mail.

Truth can be briefly expressed in a joke when a serious explanation could take many more words. A close English translation of *ceteris paribus* is "all things being equal." According to the magazine *The Economist*, economists use this phrase to "cover their backs." For example, economists might say that "higher interest rates will lead to lower inflation, *ceteris paribus*, which means that they will stand by their prediction about inflation only if nothing else changes apart from the rise in the interest rate."[25] I will never forget an economist who I associate with *The Addams Family* character, Gomez, and his articulation of *ceteris paribus*.

According to the Internet websites *Jumptheshark.com*[26] and the *BBC.com Comedy Guide,*[27]

> The sitcom *The Addams Family* ran from 1964 to 1966. The show was based on the work of Charles Addams' cartoon creations about a ghoulish family that appeared regularly in the American magazine *The New Yorker* circa 1937. John Astin was brought in to play the leading man. Gomez was a dashing, life-loving lawyer, full of *joie-de-vivre* and unfettered enthusiasm. Carolyn Jones was his darkly mysterious and sexy wife Morticia, slinking around in her figure hugging, full-length black dress. The characters were happy people who simply couldn't understand how others did not see life as they did. Gomez's affection for his 'Tish' was unbridled, and she only had to utter a French word or phrase for him to launch at her, grab her arm and plant a thousand kisses in an ascending direction until propriety or circumstance stopped him.
>
> John Astin was born on March 30, 1930 in Baltimore, Maryland. The hammy mustachioed comedic actor is best known as the character Gomez Addams. As Gomez, Astin wore a pinstriped suit, smoked cigars and stood on his head. Astin was nominated for an Oscar in 1969 for a short film he wrote, directed, and starred in, called *Prelude*.

A course in Intermediate Microeconomics as an undergraduate fired my love for the discipline. Professor White, the teacher, was a gifted economist. His *curriculum vitae* was long and distinguished, and he held great passion for academia. He was not a well-rounded man but certainly knew economics. He could also easily pass for John Astin as Gomez Addams. He even wore a heavy pinstripe with mannerisms worthy of a devoted understudy. When especially serious in making a point, he would hunch forward, wrists on hips, and swiftly but involuntarily shift his gaze from student to student. To peals of laughter from the class, one witling inquired if he was related to Astin. He was not and in fact did not know the fellow in question. On the first day of class, he captivated the students with the magic and mystery of economics. He rhapsodized about riding the curve, shifting the curve, demand, supply, optimization, marginalism, minimization, maximization and proclaimed that the Meaning of Life could be explained by economic theory. The class was captivated and of course asked the question, "Gomez, what is the Meaning of Life?" Wrists on hips, eyes shifting wildly and a knowing grin on his face, he answered, "what do you want it to be?" His mantra was "assume everything, predict nothing."

A note on all things being equal: They are not. The assumption is an analytical device used to parse models into measurable and predictable outcomes. Without the device, it would be impossible to isolate causal relationships in a complex environment. The assumption smoothes curves in a jumbled world. However, buildings do fall, markets do crash, curves do shift, input and output are lumpy. The market for pork bellies does not exist in a vacuum void of alternatives.

SaLT Concept

Always be aware of assumptions when drawing a conclusion.

CHAPTER 6

Supply and Demand

"It is very evident, that the share of the two parties is the subject of a bargain between them; and if there is a bargain, it is not difficult to see on what the terms of the bargain must depend. All bargains, when made in freedom, are determined by competition, and the terms alter according to the state of supply and demand."

—James Mill[28]

James Mill (1773-1836) was a philosopher and historian known for his belief in Utilitarianism. According to *Oxford*, "utilitarian thought" promotes the idea that the greatest happiness for the greatest number of people should be society's goal. Put another way, the individual should be willing to sacrifice, if not die, for the good of the many. Mill's older son was the Utilitarian John Stuart Mill. James Mill, born in Scotland, was educated at the University of Edinburgh. In 1814, he began writing a series of articles on politics, law and education for the *Encyclopedia Britannica*. His most celebrated work, a *History of British India*, was published in 1817. It should be noted that Mill never visited India although the work is considered profound. Mill's *Elements of Political Economy (1821)* was influenced by the work of Ricardo.[29]

"He [the individual] generally, indeed, neither intends to promote the public interest, nor knows how much he is promoting it. By preferring the support of domestic [industry] to that of foreign industry, he intends only his own security; and by directing that industry in such a manner as its produce may be of the greatest value, he intends only his own gain, and he is in this, as in many other cases, led by an invisible hand to promote an end which was no part of his intention."[30]

Smith's "invisible hand" allocates society's resources efficiently according to the laws of supply and demand, as subject to competition. The law of demand is the notion that "all things being equal," the higher a good's cost or price, the less consumers will demand or consume it. Conversely, the law of supply observes that the higher the price, the more of a good the supplier is willing to produce for sale.

Graph 6.1—Supply and Demand

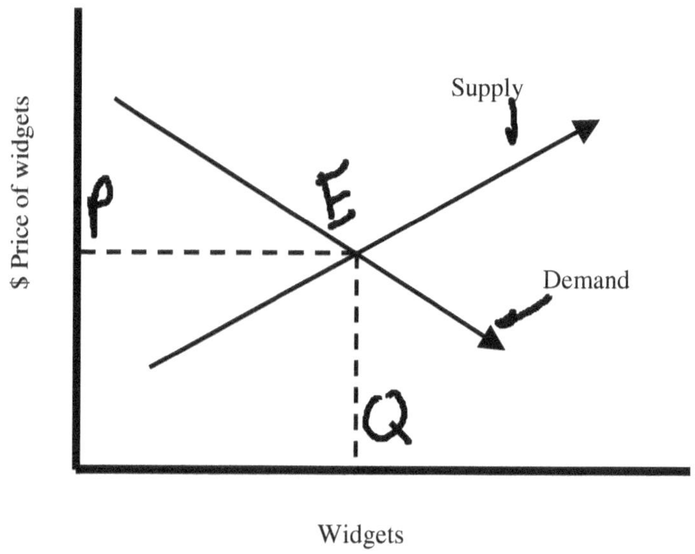

Widgets

We will use the ubiquitous "widget" for our illustration. *Oxford* defines the widget as, "any gadget or device." Gadget is defined as, "a small, ingenious device." The origin is unknown but its etymology is traced to maritime use in the 19th century. One thing is certain; economists overuse it!

In our world of widgets, the intersection of supply and demand is considered equilibrium. At equilibrium (E) all the widgets produced (Q) are consumed at price (P). At a price above P, a glut would ensue and the price would be driven down to E. At a price lower than P, a shortage would exist and the price would be driven up until equilibrium existed again. Our analysis assumes perfect competition with the following five characteristics:

1. Product sold is identical in all respects.

2. All firms are price takers with no price discrimination (no power to set price and no individual negotiation).

3. All firms have a small market share and do not control the market.

4. Buyers know the nature of the product sold and the prices charged by each firm (perfect information).

5. The industry is characterized by freedom of entry and exit (no barriers to entry such as capital, regulation, or scale).

This is also known as "pure competition." This form of competition is rare in the "real world," as meeting all five criteria is difficult. It is only useful in the *analysis* of supply and demand. Depending upon your definitions and time frame, the classification of competition can change. In a limited geography over a short period of time, the market may look like it is controlled by monopoly. Having the only snow shovel for sale during a snowstorm would be an example. In the longer run, a market dominated by a monopoly could look more like pure competition. Think of the phone company 20 years ago. Now phone service can be obtained through cable, wireless and VoIP.

Movement along the curve *versus* movement of the curve

A movement along the curve refers to a change in only price or quantity as the curve describes it. "All things are equal" along a stable curve. For instance, if the price increases, demand for the good is less. Movement along the supply curve denotes only a change in price or quantity. It does not account for changing production technology, or changing prices of inputs. Movements of the supply and demand curves are considered shifts of the curves. A shift in the curve occurs when a good's quantity demanded or supplied changes at all prices. Things are no longer equal.

Picture a world where the only goods are Belch Beer and Yakov Vodka. Two forces that can shift the demand curve for Yakov are:

1. Preferences—Yakov Vodka initiates an advertising campaign causing it to become more popular at all prices. This is an upward shift of the demand curve for Yakov.

2. Competing goods—Belch Beer has innovated its supply process and becomes more plentiful at lower prices than before. Yakov is now

demanded at a lower price at all quantities. This is a downward shift in demand for Yakov.

Two forces shifting the supply of Belch beer:

1. Technology—As above, a change in the manufacturing process causes Belch to have a lower cost structure in its production. This is an *outward* shift in supply of Belch.
2. Price of inputs rise—The prices of barley, hops wheat and energy all rise increasing the cost to manufacture Belch. This is known as an *inward* shift of the supply curve for Belch.

Graph 6.2—Yakov Vodka

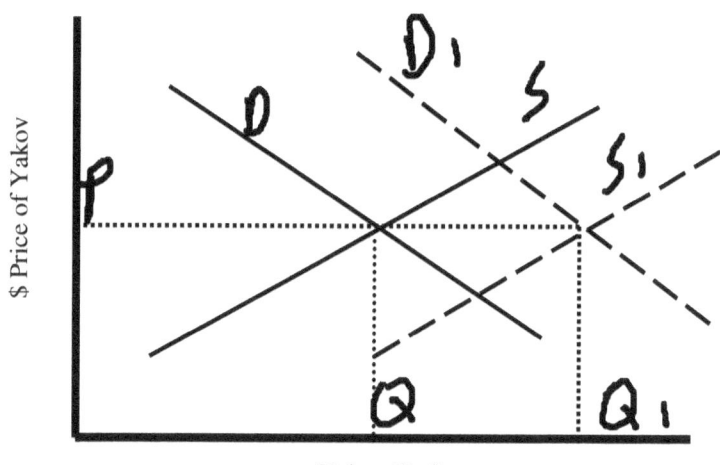

Yakov Vodka

In this graphical representation, we assume an upward shift in demand and an outward shift in supply for Yakov Vodka. In this scenario, a new equilibrium is created at the same price, but the quantity of Yakov produced and consumed has increased.

D → D1 Movement to new demand curve

S → S1 Movement to new supply curve

Q → Q1 Movement of quantity produced and consumed

P   Price remains the same

This is but one possibility of the combination of resultant prices and quantities when the curves shift.

Above we discussed how a market could be considered purely competitive or monopolistic depending on several factors including time. As we think of the real world, over time, a market could resemble both depending upon our perspective. Let's examine the market for a hypothetical commodity. The commodity will be manure.

On the continuum, the shift in the nature of competition for the hypothetical market for manure is shown below.

Graph 6.3—Competition

Characterized by monopoly

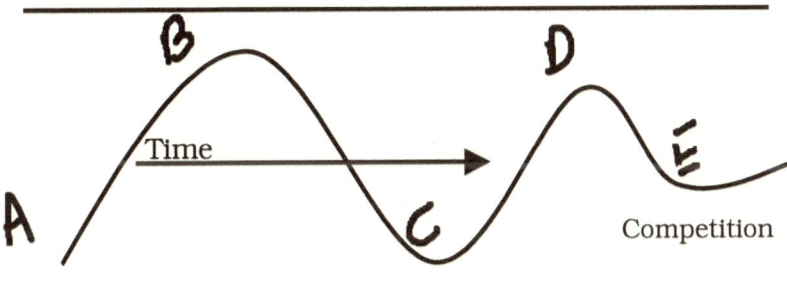

Characterized by pure competition

In our hypothetical world, manure begins as the only known fertilizer. Let's assume for argument it is horse manure of a certain shape, size and grade. At point A, manure can be purchased on any street corner, in any quantity. This would be very close to pure competition. A robber baron decided to buy all the horses in the world and sell the manure as a monopoly. This would be shown as point B. At point C, the government stepped in and broke the back of the monopoly freeing all the horses in the land so that anyone could again sell manure on any street corner. At point D, a chemist found the active chemical in manure was nitrogen and patented the process for isolation for SCAT Chemical. Point E represents the licensing of the nitrogen process to a handful of firms.

A few observations are in order about our hypothetical market for manure or fertilizer. Our characterization of market power over time is smooth as it assumes an even transformation in the continuum. At point D, the monopolistic characteristics are not as powerful as before as manure remains a fertilizer, albeit not as efficient as processed nitrogen. They are competitive goods. At point E, the market settles in to what is known as an Oligopoly that can mimic pure competition as well as a monopoly. Oligopoly will be discussed in the next chapter. Markets tend to gravitate toward oligopoly over time.

Elasticity

Elasticity refers to the slope of stable demand and supply curves, *ceteris paribus*. The steeper the absolute slope, the more inelastic the curve. Slope of the supply curve is sometimes called "sticky" or "not sticky" depending upon how fast the product can be brought to market. Stickiness is a function of the production process, distribution system and information cycle.

The main characteristic of classically elastic demand curves is that buyers are very sensitive to the changes in price.

Examples are:

1. Product is not addictive—Sliced bread
2. Product is a luxury versus a necessity—Leisure travel
3. Product has many substitutes—Coffee, tea and cola
4. Relative cost is large—Sport utility vehicle

Examples of classically inelastic demand curves where buyers are not sensitive to changes in price:

1. Product is addictive—Vodka
2. Product is a necessity—Gasoline
3. Product has no substitute—Diamonds
4. Relative cost is small—Song downloaded from iTunes

These examples are generalizations. Products can have characteristics of both types of elasticity or be inelastic at certain price levels and elastic at others. The world is more complex than eight examples. Also time and the rate of transformation can factor in elasticity.

The Real World

This concept has been referred to on more than one occasion in this text. By the "real world," I am referring to how things *really* work, not analysis from an academic or hypothetical standpoint. Academic analysis is necessary to understanding, but it does not intend to represent the real world. Mark Twain is generally credited with saying, "Climate is what we expect, weather is what we get."[31] Weather has been forecast with some level of usefulness since the 19th century.[32] Prediction of tomorrow's weather is iffy. Prediction of next week's weather is difficult. Prediction of next Tuesday's temperature, humidity, barometric pressure and precipitation is impossible! Countless supercomputers churn away at atmospheric models, yet the weather has so many interwoven variables that exact prediction becomes impossible. As American Meteorologist Edward Lorenz demonstrated with his weather models, the same process in nearly identical initial states can lead to vastly different outcomes.[33]

The real world is complex beyond comprehension. In order to make sense of it, we must use assumptions to break it into manageable parts so we can draw conclusions and try to predict what will happen. It is important for us to also remember that academic analysis suffers from what is known as the "ivory tower" effect. Academicians can become separated from realistic perspectives through seclusion. I will illustrate this by the story of the problem with consultants just to make light of my own position.

A sitcom called *Frank's Place* that aired on *CBS* in 1987 and 1988 summed it up most succinctly. The comedy, set in a New Orleans restaurant[34] served the episode titled "Night Business." Frank, played by Tim Reid, owner of the restaurant that catered to a mainly black clientele, wanted to drum up the night business. He hired a consultant to make some changes. The consultant hired a white "Cowboy" band to play and attract customers. The band struck up to the tune of "Pick a Bale of Cotton." Obviously, it was not a hit with the regulars. Bubba, portrayed by Robert Harper, the friend and confidant of Frank, said to Frank, "You know what the problem with consultants is? They know a thousand ways to make love to a woman ... problem is, they don't know any girls."

SaLT Concepts

There are many exceptions to the free market. For our purposes, four are worth note.

1. Monopoly—Exclusive control or possession in the trade of a product. Monopolies can be natural, or created by privilege or collusion. An example would be the local power company due to high barriers of entry. However, monopoly power has been hypothetically stripped by regulation.

2. Oligopoly—Limited competition between a small number of sellers. Markets tend to gravitate toward oligopolistic structures.

3. Pure competition—It rarely exists in the real world. The same is true with a pure monopoly.

4. Time—The longer the time horizon, *ceteris paribus*, on average, the flatter the curve.

Demand can be relatively elastic or inelastic. Elasticity has implications for the market.

Remember:

Avoid isolation and the loss of perspective.

CHAPTER 7

Risk

"Risk is a chance or possibility of danger, loss, injury or other adverse consequence."

—The Oxford American Dictionary

Sebastian Junger, a freelance writer who grew up in the Boston area, wrote the story of the loss at sea of the fishing boat *Andrea Gail*. The *Andrea Gail* was a long-liner that fished for Swordfish. The boat sets out miles of line with baited hooks suspended in the water. After the hooks are set, the boat hauls back the line with hopefully a good catch. The set and haul can take many hours. His book, *The Perfect Storm*, recounts the 1991 storm system that overwhelmed the fishing fleet out of Gloucester, Massachusetts in October that year. The *Andrea Gail* was lost off the coast of Nova Scotia in a storm characterized by hurricane force winds and mountainous seas. In the book, a fine articulation of risk is described as a "narrowing range of choices." The passage presented describes the last radio contact with the *Andrea Gail* with Junger's vision of the events as they unfolded. This passage does not describe risk as we generally define it in finance, but is worthwhile as we consider how risk manifests itself as we travel along the path of time.

> Billy's [*Andrea Gail's* Captain] been through a lot of storms, though, and he's probably brought her around earlier in the evening, maybe even before talking to Barrie [Billy's fellow Captain on another boat]. Either way, it's a significant moment; it means they've stopped steaming home and are simply trying to survive. In a sense Billy's no longer at the helm, the conditions are, and all he can do is react. If danger can be seen in terms of a narrowing range of choices, Billy Tyne's choices have just

racheted [sic] down a notch. A week ago he could have headed in early. A day ago he could have run north like Johnston [another fellow boat Captain]. An hour ago he could have radioed to see if there were any other vessels around. Now the electrical noise has made the VHF practically useless, and the single sideband only works for long range. These aren't mistakes so much as the inability to see into the future. No one, not even the Weather Service, knows for sure what a storm's going to do.[35]

As Junger has stated, risk increases as the range of options narrows. Measured risk is the probability of an outcome multiplied by the consequence of an outcome. Without boring ourselves with the intricacies of statistical measurement, a common risk metric is mean and standard deviation. In other words, given the average and standard deviation we could say that with 95% confidence, we expect x to occur within a range around x. Take the popularity of President Bush recently published on May 9, 2006 citing Bush's job approval rating at 31%. What does this mean exactly?

According to the *Gallup Poll News Service*, Gallop took a sample poll of Americans, 1,013 national adults, 18 or older via telephone May 5-7, 2006, and asked, "Do you approve or disapprove of the way George W. Bush is handling his job as President?" Based upon their results and the magic of statistical analysis, they make the following statement about the nation as a whole.[36]

With 95% confidence, 31% of Americans, 18 or older, approve of Bush's handling of affairs plus or minus 3%. So with virtual certainty, 28% to 34% of Americans approve of Bush. This illustrates how mean and standard deviation is used given a level of variance. Variance denoting how disparate, in our case, a result can be. In terms of investing in the stock market, a similar term, "volatility," is measured by "beta."

Volatility is the measure of a stock's movement versus the market as a whole as measured by beta. The higher the volatility, the riskier the stock. Beta is basically the change in the stock price divided by the change in price in the market. A beta greater than 1 means the stock is more volatile than the market. A beta of less than one means the stock is less volatile than the market.

Frank Knight establishes the difference between risk and uncertainty. He says, "… risk means in some cases a quantity susceptible of measurement; [and] it will appear that a measurable uncertainty or a risk proper, as we shall use the term is so far different from an unmeasurable one that [the unmeasurable] is not in effect an uncertainty at all."[37] From this we can grasp that Knight does not consider something that can't be measured as a risk as surely as a certain outcome does not pose a risk. Jumping from an airplane without a parachute is not a risk. It is a certainty of death. An event that we are not aware of, assuming due diligence, lurking in the future is not a risk. The risk of a total market meltdown, a *coup d'état*, global death and destruction are not measurable uncertainties.

The Basel Committee has played a leading role in standardizing international bank regulations across jurisdictions in order to promote monetary stability. The Basel Committee on Banking Supervision is comprised of representatives from central banks and their regulatory authorities.

The committee identified several areas of loss events and ways to minimize risks associated with those events. The areas they identify are: Internal and external fraud; employment practices and workplace safety; client's products and business practice; damage to physical assets; business disruption and systems failures; execution, delivery and process management.[38]

In recent years, the Federal Reserve also required U.S. banks to undertake planning for disaster recovery. While contingency planning can be useful, and notwithstanding recent tragedies such as 9/11/2001 and Hurricane Katrina where people performed extraordinary acts, catastrophe falls into the category of unmeasurable and deemed not a risk in the proper sense. Some disaster recovery plans at major corporations border, if not tread upon, the absurd. A few examples at a large commercial bank that I was affiliated with illustrate this point.

According to the plan, "In the event of computer system failure caused by a global virus affecting local systems and the Internet as a whole," the bank required that "Commercial lending officers should remain at their desks to meet customer needs such as wiring funds." What is absurd? You can't wire funds without electronic access to the Federal Reserve System.

In the event of "A collapse of the Federal Reserve System" bank tellers, "should be prepared to manually issue deposit receipts using index cards and an official rubber stamp." What is absurd? If the Federal Reserve were to collapse, check clearing, withdrawals and deposits would most likely cease in all cases.

In the event of, "The physical destruction of headquarters, staff should work from home using duplicate files stored in the trunk of their vehicle." What is absurd? Ignoring the risk of storing sensitive files in an unsecured automobile, one group to follow this mandate was the Marketing Department. I suppose there is a benefit in pondering how to capitalize on the institution's success in recovering from a disaster, but it is not an immediate problem to be addressed!

In the paper, "Defining Risk," Glyn A. Holton defines the term Operationalism. As knowledge stems from experience, definitions are only meaningful if they refer to experiences. Therefore, we can only "operationalize" our perception of risk. The author theorizes, "… manageable task is to operationally define some aspects of perceived risk. Risk metrics, such as variance of return, are used for this purpose. It is meaningless to ask if a risk metric captures risk. Instead, ask if it is useful."[39]

In the scope of this book we are concerned with achieving our goals. I term the risk of achievement "execution risk" inherent in our plans. A very simple illustration of execution risk follows:

Consider the two scenarios to accomplish the same goal. Because of an important meeting the next day, it is imperative that you attend the scheduled event promptly at 8:00 am.

Scenario A—The night before you fill your car with gas, pack the kid's lunch, plan to wake 30 minutes early setting two alarm clocks and leave home in double the time needed to travel to the office.

Scenario B—You forget to set the alarm, have to be creative in packing the kid's lunch, discover that your car is out of gas and leave your home at the last possible moment in order to arrive on time without regard to traffic snarls.

Which Scenario has a greater chance of a negative outcome? The simpler the plan, the less execution risk.

What are the ways to reduce your execution risk in terms of SaLT?

Figure 7.1—Execution Risk and SaLT

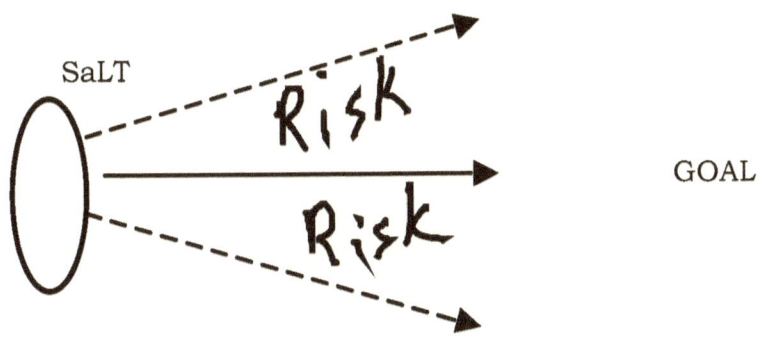

In order to minimize your execution risk you want to do three things:

1. Have a clear, well-defined goal with appropriate strategy, logistics and tactics. These items will be discussed in later chapters.

2. As illustrated by Junger's definition of risk, maximize your choices, or put another way, maximize control of the variables.

3. All things being equal, minimize the complexity of your plan.

The figure above denotes areas of execution risk given a clear, well-defined goal with corresponding SaLT.

As illustrated by the film *A Simple Plan* (1998), even simple plans can go wrong. A simple plan may not be as simple as it seems.

Two brothers played by Bill Paxton and Billy Bob Thorton and a friend find $4.4 million inside a crashed plane in the wilderness of northern Ohio. The three men conspire to keep the find a secret and steal the money for themselves. They suspect the money and plane are part of drug running so no one will legitimately miss the plane, or more importantly, its cargo of cash. The three men find themselves at odds with one another on how long to sit on the loot and ultimately how each should go about spending his share. The trust between the three slowly dissolves with "accidents" starting to happen and a nosy FBI officer to deal with. In the end, the money is worthless and the main character ponders how he and the others could do such evil things.[40]

SaLT Concept

Minimize execution risk by having a simple plan and maximize control of the variables.

CHAPTER 8

Oligopoly and Game Theory

An oligopoly is a market form that is dominated by a small number of firms. Because there are few participants in this type of market, each is aware of the action of the others. The decisions of one firm influences, and is influenced by, the decision of others. The product or services the firms offer are differentiated often branded and secure since barriers to entry are high. Following from intense price competitiveness, firms often utilize non-price competition in order to increase revenue and market share. An oligopolistic structure can give rise to a wide range of different outcomes. In some situations, the firms may wish to collude in order to raise prices and restrict production in the same way as a monopoly can. Firms desire to collude in an attempt to stabilize markets, which reduces the risks inherent in these markets for investment and product development. Where there is a formal agreement for collusion, it is usually illegal. In some industries, there may be a market leader, which informally sets prices to which other producers respond. This is known as price leadership.[41]

Sophisticated firms anticipating rivals' behavior might appear to act in concert through conscious parallelism[42] or imitation by a business of a competitor's action, such as changing price without active conspiracy between business rivals. It has been estimated that 25% of Gross Domestic Product is attributed to oligopolistic structures.[43] While oligopolistic firms can theoretically raise prices, arguments have been made that oligopolies have positive benefits for the economy as a whole, such as increasing production efficiencies, putting price pressure on suppliers and pressuring wages. The airline and automobile industries are prime examples of oligopolies. There is also a tendency for all industries to move toward an oligopolistic structure through consolidation in order to reap greater market share and profit versus pure competition. While many small businesses do not pass all the criteria of an oligopoly, most do have to consider competitor's actions. A tremendous base of knowledge has been developed over time to model a rival's actions.

The Prisoner's Dilemma

The Prisoner's Dilemma depicts two partners in crime confronted with the following choices. If one confesses and the other does not, the confessor receives a short sentence and the other goes to jail for a long time. If neither confesses, each goes free. If both confess, each goes to jail for a short period of time. Each reasons that he is better off confessing because if the other confesses, he receives a short sentence by confessing and a long sentence by not confessing. Since each rationalizes this way, each confesses, and so each is given a short sentence; whereas if each had not confessed, each would have gone free. The prisoner's decision is affected by the decision of the other. While each could have gone free by not confessing, each prisoner acts in his own best interest to minimize his sentence by his own actions. Albert Tucker popularized the notion of the Prisoner's Dilemma.

> Albert William Tucker was chair of Princeton University's Mathematics Department and originator of the influential paradox known as the "Prisoner's Dilemma." Tucker began his career in mathematics as a topologist, and is best known for his pioneering work in linear programming and game theory. He was a mentor to the generation of mathematicians who studied at Princeton from 1940 to 1970.
>
> In 1950, while addressing an audience of psychologists at Stanford University, where he was a visiting professor, Tucker created the Prisoner's Dilemma to illustrate the difficulty of analyzing non-zero-sum games (scenarios in which one contestant's victory is not necessarily the other contestant's defeat). Tucker's simple paradox has since given rise to a vast literature in subjects as diverse as philosophy, biology, sociology, political science, and economics, as well as game theory itself.[44]

Table 8.1—Prisoner's Dilemma

	Prisoner B stays silent	Prisoner B confesses
Prisoner A stays silent	Both go free	B gets short sentence A gets long sentence
Prisoner A confesses	A gets short sentence B gets long sentence	Both serve short sentence

There is no "right" solution to this game because outcome is influenced independently by each party. One cannot be confident of what the other will do. This analysis assumes the crooks are "ordinary," that is they do not trust each other. In this scenario, the best outcome would be for neither to confess and both go free due to lack of evidence. Once uncertainty is factored in, the best individual action is to confess.

Let's take two firms with identical goods charging identical "prices." Price includes all non-price competition. The two firms can attempt to raise, lower or keep price the same.

If both firms let existing prices remain the same, nothing will change. They will keep present market share and the share of resultant profits. If one lowers price and the other does not, the firm lowering price will capture market share and the resultant profit associated with it. If both lower price, each will suffer, not from a changing share of the market, but from a smaller pool of profit to capture. Ignoring the mathematical proof, if one firm lowers price the other will follow suit resulting in a worse outcome for both. This is the classical price war. Conversely, if one firm attempts to unilaterally raise price, he will suffer from a smaller market share and lower profit if the other firm does not match his higher price. Rationally, he would return to price at the competitor's price. Given the motive to "cheat" *vis-à-vis* the competitor is high, it is difficult to raise prices in this market structure.

This gives rise to the Nash Equilibrium.[45]

John Forbes Nash, Jr. (b.1928) is an American mathematician working in game theory and differential geometry. He shared the 1994 Nobel Prize in Economics for his work in the field. He is best known in popular culture as the subject of the Hollywood movie, *A Beautiful Mind*, about his mathematical genius and his struggles with mental illness. Born in Bluefield, West Virginia, he received his undergraduate and graduate degrees from Carnegie in mathematics and completed his doctorate at Princeton and formed his theory of equilibrium in "Non-cooperative Games" in 1951. The thesis was written under the supervision of Albert Tucker and has become known as the Nash Equilibrium. The theory attempts to explain the dynamics of threat and reaction among competitors.[46]

The Nash Equilibrium is an optimal collective strategy in a game involving two or more players, where no player has anything to gain by only changing his or her own strategy. If each player has chosen a strategy and no player can benefit by changing his or her strategy while the other players keep theirs unchanged, then the current set of strategy choices and the corresponding payoffs constitute a Nash Equilibrium. These choices are considered sustainable.[47] Nash's results hinge on assumptions central to economics, especially the notion that people behave rationally and act in their own self-interest.

Let's examine a real world example to see the equilibrium in action. First, imagine two dry cleaners operating across a busy street. One abuts to an affluent neighborhood, the other to a lesser-income neighborhood. They each offer the same competent service and offer no real distinction in product. I have chosen this scenario for three reasons: Dry cleaning seemingly represents a free market; it represents a quintessential small business, and it illustrates how important geographical considerations can be. It is a free market with one exception that is very similar to real world constraints. The cleaners must take into account the other's action.

Figure 8.1—Our Dry Cleaning Micro-market

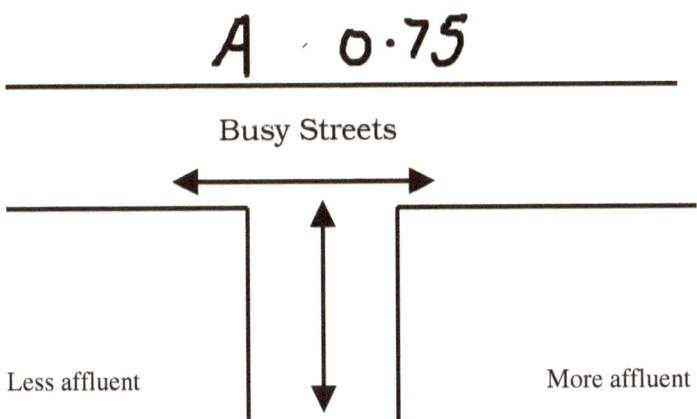

A   0·75

Busy Streets

Less affluent

More affluent

1.00

1.25

Sparkle
Cleaners

Dazzle Cleaners

Sparkle Cleaners serves the less affluent neighborhood and Dazzle the more affluent. Currently, Sparkle charges $1.00 per shirt and Dazzle $1.25 per shirt. Dazzle's customers, being more affluent, will pay a bit more for cleaning instead of crossing a busy street to save $0.25. The cliché "location, location, location" is often used by those that make their business in the real estate industry. It is also true of businesses, especially retail, tied to a particular tract of land. In a particular local market, a shift from one street corner to the next, while seemingly nominal, can make the difference between success and failure. For example, in Tulsa, there is an imaginary line called the Red River that divides mid-town and south Tulsa. This imaginary line is named for the Red River proper, which divides Texas from Oklahoma. Folks in the area would not think of crossing this line to shop, even though there exists in absolute terms, no difference from north of the line to south of the line. Socioeconomic and demographic factors, *et cetera* are virtually the same. A real estate developer must be extremely conscious of this phenomenon.

Dazzle and Sparkle exist in equilibrium with their markets and pricing defined. Any arbitrary change by one would elicit a response by the other to the detriment of both. If Dazzle charged more it would lose market share to Sparkle as people would be lured across the busy street to save money. If Dazzle charged less, it could lure Sparkle's customers to cross the street resulting in a new price war. Any scenario, unless they both raised prices simultaneously, would result in lower profit for both. Because of the lure of cheating, they would not raise price in unison. The Nash Equilibrium holds. There is no reason to change their pricing strategies.

Sparkle existed 5 years before Dazzle and charged $1.75 per shirt. Dazzle entered this market as it was under-served and charged less than Sparkle to lure customers. At first a price war ensued with each charging much below equilibrium, but eventually their new market stabilized and they settled into equilibrium pricing at $1.75 and $1.50 for Dazzle and Sparkle respectively.

Two years ago, a third dry cleaner opened for business at Point A in Figure 8.1. It offered super cheap pricing and its intent was to draw from a larger area through its location and bargain pricing. Super Cleaner charges $0.75 per shirt since it opened. Their business is brisk and the model is sound. Before Super Cleaners opened, Dazzle and Sparkle charged $1.75 and $1.50 respectively. When Super opened, Dazzle and Sparkle were faced with a challenge to their strategic choices in pricing. They were both losing customers to Super. They both had to lower prices enough to offset the customers desire to save against the extra trouble to brave traffic to patronize Super. Dazzle and Sparkle now exist again in equilibrium at $1.25 and $1.00 respectively. Super, Sparkle and Dazzle all exist in equilibrium and will most likely stay that way unless some event or outside competitor changes the landscape. It should be recognized that Sparkle made more money before Dazzle came along. Sparkle and Dazzle made more money before Super came along. Super, Sparkle and Dazzle now are all part of the same micro-market dividing a limited pie.

Is Cooperation Precluded From Economic Systems?

Martin A. Nowak, Robert M. May and Karl Sigmund, in the article, "The Arithmetic's of Mutual Help," examined cooperation using a Prisoner's Dilemma model to illustrate cooperation in evolution. They modeled evolution with successive generations of "prisoners" to determine if the system would generate cooperation as witnessed in nature. The authors cite many examples of cooperative animal behavior in nature: grooming, feeding, teaching, warning and cooperative hunting, to name a few. The classical outcome of the Prisoner's Dilemma is for participants to defect, *i.e.* not cooperate. In their experiments, players participate in round robin tournaments earning points for outcome and creating "prodigy" that behave as they do in successive tournaments. Four basic strategies of play were modeled. "Always cooperate, always defect, tit-for-tat, Pavlov." Always cooperate and defect strategies are self-explanatory. "Tit-for-tat begins with a cooperative response and then repeats the opposing player's previous move." The Pavlov rule sticks with the former move if it has a high payoff, but switches if the last move brought a low payoff; in other words, "win-stay," "lose-shift." While this research drew numerous conclusions, for our purpose it discovered that systems were characterized by neither cooperation nor defection, but over time a system would evolve toward cooperative behavior. The collapse of the system, while rare, could be abrupt. Even though cooperation increased over time, the threat of "sudden collapse" always loomed, especially if outside events were encountered.[48]

Non-Price Competition

Oligopolistic industries, or more accurately, businesses that consider rival's actions, by their nature rely on non-price competition to differentiate their product. Non-price competition can take many forms such as branding, actual product differentiation and incentives. Coke and Pepsi, Mac and Windows, Green Stamps from yesteryears and airline miles are all examples. David Leonhardt wrote in the *New York Times* on the history of Green Stamps, AAdvantage, and non-price competition.[49]

American Airlines, in response to industry deregulation began its frequent flier program on May 1, 1981. It was christened AAdvantage and based on the model of S&H Green Stamps as a way to increase customer loyalty without reducing airfare. According to the *Economist*, there are 14 trillion unredeemed miles in all miles programs. With a theoretical value of $0.01 per mile, the value exceeds all U.S. currency in circulation. Green Stamps ultimately failed in part because retailers reached the conclusion that they could offer discounts more economically than the cost of the Green Stamp program. As intended, airline miles delayed the erosion of fares. "One study done in the 1990's found that business travelers taking a 1,000-mile trip would pay an extra $170.00 on average to fly an airline with their frequent flier program."

Current wisdom has placed miles in a category with Green Stamps late in their cycle. Miles are no longer used exclusively to fly a particular carrier, but can be used to purchase almost any product. The tendency of the airlines to cause miles to be particularly difficult to redeem for flights and upgrades has quickened this trend.

S&H Green Stamps were a popular consumer incentive originated by the Sperry & Hutchinson Company in 1896.[50] At its peak in the 1950's and 1960's, the program was a widely recognized American cultural icon. Immortalized in American culture by the ABC television show, *The Brady Bunch,* in episode "54-40 and Fight," in which the boys have 40 books of stamps and the girls 54. Neither has enough to trade for what they want so the dispute is settled by building a house of cards. Before the contest is completed, the dog, Tiger, upsets the contest. In a heartwarming show of cooperation, the kids opt for a trade the whole family can enjoy: A color television.[51]

The hope was that people would seek out merchants distributing Green Stamps and stay loyal to them. When you collected enough stamps, you visited a redemption center in the local area and traded in the booklet for goods. By the 1960's a gas station or grocery store could not get by without distributing Green Stamps. In the 1970's, merchants found that the stamps were no longer an effective tool for maintaining customer loyalty. The last store to offer physical Green Stamps was a Piggly Wiggly in Tennessee, which ceased their distribution on February 14, 2003.[52]

SaLT Concepts

Oligopolistic market structures are common in our economy and rely on product differentiation whether it takes the form of branding or actual product differentiation. Non-price competition is common. It is the exception that a business can ignore its rival's actions in defining its own behavior. The Prisoner's Dilemma describes how competitors will react when the decision of one is affected by the decision of another. The Nash Equilibrium describes how competing firms will stabilize their action and not act arbitrarily unless outside events or other factors disturb the equilibrium point. Cooperation is not excluded in the market place, but as in nature, it can abruptly disintegrate. Non-price competition can stave off direct price competition, but at some point direct pricing competitiveness will result.

Remember

Be aware of your competitor's actions and behave appropriately. Arbitrary behavior is usually detrimental to all involved.

CHAPTER 9

Rationality and Choice
Under Uncertainty

"The origin of ... action is choice, and that of choice is desire and reasoning with a view to an end."

—Aristotle (384-322 BCE)—Greek philosopher who
profoundly influenced Western thought.[53]

"Rational behavior requires theory. Reactive behavior requires only reflex action."

—Attributed to W. Edwards Deming.

Deming was known as the father of the Japanese post-war industrial revival and was regarded by many as the leading quality guru in the United States.[54]

Are the following acts rational?

Selling sex or not; using sex to sell; using an addictive product; selling an addictive product; buying a certain stock; selling a certain stock now; slacking at your job; engaging in risky activities; buying a big house; living well inside your means; taking the bus; driving a fancy car; taking advantage of a stranger; feeding the homeless; giving to charity; treating your pet like a person; cheating on your spouse. Whatever the choice, is it rational? Irrational?

One person's choice may not be yours, "but it cannot, by itself, be irrational."[55]

Rationality in economics and choice theory means acting in terms of one's desires. It does not consider whether those desires are in and of themselves "rational." *Oxford* defines "rational" as, "sensible, sane, moderate." This is not rationality as economics refers to it. In economics, rational behavior requires that individuals maximize utility under the constraints they face. The concept of rational behavior has two parts. First, it allows us to derive optimal economic behavior in a "normative" sense. That is, determine what is reasonable in an economic framework. Second, models of rational behavior can be used to explain and predict actual behavior. Thus, one ponders a rational allocation of resources, or a rational corporate strategy. In this concept of rationality, the goals or motives are taken for granted and not subject to criticism, ethical or otherwise. Thus, rationality simply refers to the success of goal attainment, whatever those goals may be.

Leonard J. Savage (1917-1971) was an American mathematician and statistician graduated from the University of Michigan. His most noted work was the 1954 book *Foundations of Statistics*, in which he put forward a theory of subjective probability and statistics.

The Theory of Subjective Utility is a central element of rational decision making. Its basic assumption is that choices are made among a given set of alternatives with probability distributions of outcomes for each alternative in such a way as to maximize the expected value of a given utility function.[56] The alternatives and probabilities are what the observer believes them to be.[57] In other words, probability is subjective versus objective when factoring uncertainty.

Blaise Pascal (1623-1662) was a French mathematician, physicist, and religious philosopher. In mathematics, Pascal helped create two major new areas of research. He wrote on the subjects of geometry and probability and influenced the development of economics. Following a mystical experience, he devoted himself to philosophy and theology. Two of his most famous works are *Les Provinciales* and *Pensées*.[58] From *Pensées* he says:

"Let us weigh the gain and the loss in wagering that God is. Let us estimate the two chances. If you gain, you gain all; if you lose, you lose nothing. Wager, then without hesitation that He is."[59]

Pascal's wager is a classic example of a choice under uncertainty. The uncertainty, according to Pascal, is whether or not God exists. The belief or not in God is a choice to be made. However, the reward for belief in God if God actually does exist is infinite. Therefore; however small the probability of God's existence, the expected value of belief exceeds that of non-belief, so it is better to believe in God.[60]

Thomas Bayes (1702-1761) was a British mathematician and Presbyterian minister, known for having formulated his theorem, which was published posthumously. He published two works in his lifetime: *Divine Benevolence; or, An Attempt to Prove That the Principal End of the Divine Providence and Government is the Happiness of His Creatures* (1731), and *An Introduction to the Doctrine of Fluxions, and a Defence of the Mathematicians Against the Objections of the Author of the Analyst* (published anonymously in 1736).[61]

Bayes defines probability as follows:

"The probability of any event is the ratio between the value at which an expectation depending on the happening of the event ought to be computed, and the chance of the thing expected upon it's [sic] happening"[62]

For example, given a specified number of white and black balls in a jar, what is the probability of drawing a black ball? Given that one or more balls have been drawn, what can be said about the number of white and black balls remaining in the jar? Bayes' theory of inverse or subjective probability approaches this problem in this way:

Probability of getting black ball = expected number of black balls remaining divided by total number of balls remaining.

His theory updates probability for the belief that an occurrence will happen in light of new information. Inherent in his work is the notion that we believe a proposition to be true. In other words, our experience of the makeup of distribution of the balls in the jar in the past is indicative of the future.

In utility theory we would say that expected utility is the probability of an event multiplied by the payoff received in case of that event.

Expected Utility = Probability of an event multiplied by Payoff of an event.

As in Pascal's case, we should choose a path that leads to the greatest utility. However, our judgment of probability and payoff are subject to the extent of our knowledge and what we consider to be true. This gives rise to many instances of decision bias.

Biases are anomalies in rational economic decision making related to the way we perceive reality. In researching the subject, I found no fewer than twenty-five easily recognizable biases. For our purposes, three will be discussed that are closely related:

> Status Quo Bias—An option is more desirable because it is the status quo and for no other reason. Inertia prevents movement away from the status quo. We prefer the way things are.[63]

> The Endowment Effect—People place a higher value on objects they own relative to objects they do not. In one experiment, people demanded a higher price for a coffee mug that had been given to them, but put a lower price on one they did not yet own.[64]

> Loss Aversion—Tendency for people to strongly prefer avoiding losses rather than acquiring gains. Some studies suggest that losses are twice as psychologically powerful as gains.[65]

In each of the biases cited above, a bird in hand is worth two in the bush. The origin of this idiom seems to originate from Aesop's Fables.

Aesop, famous for his fables, was arguably a slave of African descent who lived from 620 to 560 BCE in Ancient Greece. Little was known about him from credible records, except that he was at one point freed from slavery and that he eventually died in the hands of the Delphians. In fact, the obscurity shrouding his life has led some scholars to question his existence altogether.[66] Aesop wrote the following fables:

The Hawk and the Nightingale[67]

> A Nightingale sitting aloft upon an oak and singing according to his wont, was seen by a Hawk who, being in need of food, swooped down and seized him. The Nightingale, about to lose his life, earnestly begged the Hawk to let him go, saying that he was not big enough to satisfy the hunger of a Hawk who, if he wanted food, ought to pursue the larger birds.

The Hawk, interrupting him, said: "I should indeed have lost my senses if I should let go food ready in my hand, for the sake of pursuing birds which are not yet even within sight."

The Politicians[68]

An Old Politician and a Young Politician were traveling through a beautiful country, by the dusty highway which leads to the City of Prosperous Obscurity. Lured by the flowers and the shade and charmed by the songs of birds which invited to woodland paths and green fields, his imagination fired by glimpses of golden domes and glittering palaces in the distance on either hand, the Young Politician said: "Let us, I beseech thee, turn aside from this comfortless road leading, thou knowest whither, but not I. Let us turn our backs upon duty and abandon ourselves to the delights and advantages which beckon from every grove and call to us from every shining hill. Let us, if so thou wilt, follow this beautiful path, which, as thou seest, hath a guide-board saying, 'Turn in here all ye who seek the Palace of Political Distinction.'"

"It is a beautiful path, my son," said the Old Politician, without either slackening his pace or turning his head, "and it leadeth among pleasant scenes. But the search for the Palace of Political Distinction is beset with one mighty peril." "What is that?" said the Young Politician. "The peril of finding it," the Old Politician replied, pushing on.

As distinguished from our biases above, bias in the perception of risk can be depicted graphically by a S-shaped curve.

Graph 9.1—S-shaped Curve in Perception of Risk

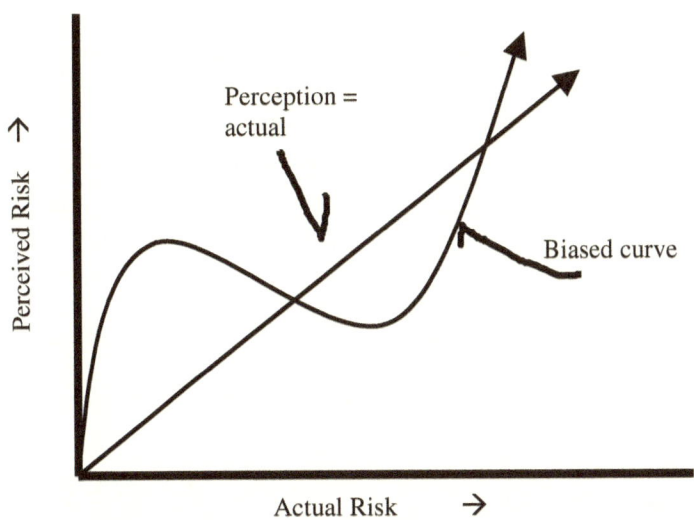

In this graph of perceived risk versus actual risk, the curved line represents our basket of biases and the straight line where actual and perceived risks are the same. On the biased line we may overweigh risk that has a low probability of occurring and underweigh outcomes with a high probability of occurrence. An example would be the risk of dying in a plane crash. Statistically this has a very low probability of occurrence, yet it is an overwhelming fear in our society. Riding in a car is an instance where the risk of injury is quite high relative to air travel, but we tend to discount this risk. The shape of the biased curve in Graph 9.1 is but one of many representations of bias in the perception of risk. A curve where we undervalue low probabilities and overvalue high probabilities is also possible as discussed below.

Vilfredo Pareto (1848-1923) was an Italian economist and sociologist remembered for his contributions to mathematics and economics. In his *Cours d'économie politique* (1896-1897) he articulated his theory of income distribution, which surmised a pattern of accumulation of wealth.[69] The popular, modern Pareto Principle that bears his name surmises that 80% of wealth is held by 20% of society. This is also known as the 80-20 Rule. It has been used in popular writings to explain vast phenomena of occurrences. To name a few 80-20isms: 80% of sales come from 20% of your efforts, 80% of complaints arise from 20% of your products, 80% of problems are related to a 20% of customers, 80% correct is perfection, *et cetera.*

In terms of how people perceive risk, Clifford Konold studied informally assessing probability.[70] I always associate this work with my own perception and have coined it the "70% rule" in honor of Pareto. In assessing the probability of an outcome, I tend to group ranges of probability into three different categories:

> It will happen—70% or above
>
> Don't know—30% to 70%
>
> It will not happen—Less than 30%

Figure 9.1—Grouping of Probability

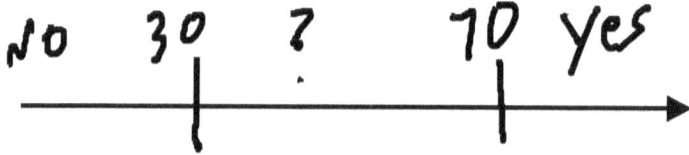

Along the continuum of probability → 0 to 100%

This means, at least to me, an event with less than a 30% chance of manifesting will be perceived as no risk of occurrence. 30% to 70% percent is a gray area where something may or may not happen. Above 70% is considered a certainty. We could argue about the breaks, but we all fall somewhere on the continuum. Again, think for a moment about the weather. A 20% chance of rain goes unheeded. A 50% chance and you could get wet. An 80% chance and you grab your umbrella before leaving home. You will have to assess for yourself where the breaks are.

Many economists view bias as irrational behavior. As seen by the S-shaped curve, the utility function can be shaped differently as our biases are added. Irrationality may not be so at all, but merely more complicated rational behavior than simple models can demonstrate. Remember that the idea of economic analysis is to hold one variable constant while chang-ing another to predict behavior. If the utility function has many dimen-sions, it would not be conducive to simplistic analysis. However, if we add more variables, the usefulness of the analysis disappears into complexity.

Satisficing is a term used in respect to bounded rationality that means get-ting a result that is good enough but is not necessarily the best.

Herbert Alexander Simon (1901-1985) was social scientist awarded the Nobel Prize in Economics for his work in Bounded Rationality. He sur-mised that getting information is costly and outcomes can't always be known, so people don't maximize utility but "satisfice." They do as well as they think is possible.[71]

"What information consumes is rather obvious: it consumes the attention of its recipients. Hence a wealth of information creates a poverty of atten-tion, and a need to allocate that attention efficiently among the overabun-dance of information sources that might consume it."[72]

As an analyst, I worked closely with a senior lender named Jock Braddock. Jock was in his early 50's and had phenomenal perspective. He was also, like me, a big picture guy. He had a couple of favorite sayings that he would bark at me if he felt I had lost sight of what was important. He seemed to have a fascination with old shoes. When he was mildly irritated he would say, "Blake, I have shoes older than you." I kept imagining a worn pair of white bucks. I think he was pointing out that he had a wealth of experience beyond mine, which I will grant him. When he was really irritated he would bark, "Blake, stop gazing at your navel!" Apparently navel-gazing was one of the seven deadly sins in his book. To navel-gaze is to stare complacently at one's navel while overlooking the main point as you drown in information. It was quite common for him to bark this at not only me, but also anyone who committed the unpardonable sin. I think his point is worth taking as we are overwhelmed with information in our lives; it is easy to lose perspective. A specialist exists for almost every discipline down to breeding habits for falcons. It takes effort not to be overwhelmed and suffer poverty of attention.

In addition to being a fine banker, Jock was also an avid falconer. He often spoke of his falcons including how he fed them and facilitated their breed-ing. To feed the birds, lest he unleash them on an unsuspecting duck, he bought dozens of young chickens, called pullets, and wrung their necks to kill them, and stored his harvest in a freezer for the hungry falcons. He also showed me a picture of his breeding helmet. I assume this was home constructed for falcon semen collection. It was a football helmet with a facemask and a perch on the top with a basin for fluids. Jock said he would wear the helmet near a donor, flap his arms and the bird would "mount" on top of the helmet. It was all I could do to keep from getting the giggles while listening to this tale. Jock also had another phrase that he liked to bark at me. He would say that, "I'd never risked it (meaning had money at risk), but he had and never lost a dime." To this day, if especially anxious, I have this recurring dream of Jock wearing his helmet, flapping his arms, killing pullets and bellowing to a Gilbert and Sullivan tune:

> You've never risked it,
> Laid it on the line.
> I'm Jock Braddock,
> I've never lost a dime!

The last project that Jock and I worked on was a company that sold small "e." "e" stood for energy in general but in this specific transaction "e" stood for electricity. Some fellows from Houston were seeking transactional financing to buy and sell "e" and make a lot of "m" or money. We spent several hours with this group, and I easily understood trading oil and gas in a pipeline, but electricity required higher level thinking. No time for navel-gazing!

Crowley's Ridge is the most distinctive feature of the landscape of southeast Missouri and northeast Arkansas, rising inland 90 miles from the Mississippi River at Memphis. In 1811-12, the New Madrid Earthquake laid waste a large part of the area that would become Greene County, Arkansas. Previous quakes over time have been credited with changing the course of the Mississippi River and creating or exposing the ridge. The New Madrid quake is now judged to have been of intensity geologists characterize as total destruction. The quake affected a three-state area, and for years was a scene of desolation which delayed settlement by at least a decade. The earth sank in places 15 to 20 feet, and rose in others, destroying the channel of the St. Francis River.[73]

In the spring of 1821, Benjamin Crowley, a 65-year old surveyor and a holder of a New Madrid Land Certificate, left his home in Kentucky in the company of his two older sons and several slaves seeking suitable land on which to settle with his wife and 8 children. They crossed the

Mississippi at Cairo and came down the ridge to the Missouri line into Lawrence County and stopped at Davidsonville. They stopped there long enough to plant a crop and then proceeded down the ridge, which was to bear the Crowley name.

When the party reached a large spring, which had been used for many years by Indians for their gatherings, the elder Crowley is reported to have said to his sons, "this is good enough." He had located a choice spot at these springs which are now part of Crowley State Park, located about 12 miles west of Paragould, Arkansas.[74] Crowley had satisficed. He found land teeming with water, flora, fauna and friendly natives: a perfectly suitable place to locate his clan. He needed to search no further.

SaLT Concepts

Understand your decision making process and be aware of your own biases. In the real world, we satisfice due to limitations of information, experience and knowledge of outcomes. Satisficing is a necessary evil. Gathering too much information can lead to inaction, which is also a choice to not act. However, ignorance does not lead to an optimal outcome either.

Chapter 10

Time, Timing and Time Frame

Ticking away the moments that make up a dull day
You fritter and waste the hours in an off hand way
Kicking around on a piece of ground in your home town
Waiting for someone or something to show you the way

—From "Time." lyrics by Roger Waters[75]

The Native American dream catcher is a webbed hoop with a hole in the center that is placed above one who is sleeping. The origin and purpose differ from one tribe to another. Desiring not to offend any particular tribe, in general, I will simply state that the dream catcher separates good dreams and bad. As dreams are a way for the Great Spirit to communicate, the dream catcher sorts ideas or wisdom. Good ideas can be captured in one's dreams and the bad allowed to pass through. Or conversely, bad dreams could be captured and the good pass to the dreamer. One interpretation envisions good thoughts passing through and the bad held until a more propitious time when the dreamer can learn from the message.

Using the dream catcher as an example, time could be like a wheel, or time could be like a river. If you miss an opportunity it will come back around, or an opportunity missed could never return again. Time could also just be time and pass with no meaning.

"… I was in time again, hearing the watch. It was Grandfather's and when Father gave it to me he said I give you the mausoleum of all hope and desire; it's rather excruciating-ly apt that you will use it to gain the *reducto absurdum* of all human experience which can fit your individual needs no better than it fitted his or his father's. I give it to you not that you may remember time, but that you might forget it now and then for a moment and not spend all your breath trying to conquer it. Because no battle is ever won he said. They are not even fought. The field only reveals to man his own folly and despair, and victory is an illusion of philosophers and fools."

—Quentin Compson, June 10, 1910[76]

Time value of money

Given a required rate of return, you would be indifferent receiving $1 today or $1 plus "interest" tomorrow. For instance, if your required rate of return is 10%, you would be indifferent between $1 today or $1.10 a year from now. The equation to calculate the future value of $1 is:

Future value = Present value multiplied by (1+required return) raised by the number of periods.

Conversely the Present value = Future value divided by (1+required return) raised by the number of periods.

In a similar fashion we can calculate the present or future value of a stream of payments or an annuity, calculate mortgage payments or net present value of investment in an asset, *et cetera*. Knowing the income stream and the required rate of return to apply are the tricks. Usually the required return is thought of as the yield. Theoretically the yield for a company should exceed its cost of capital. For example, consider the only source of capital for a company as a bank loan with and interest rate of x%. If the company wished to buy an asset it should, on a risk-adjusted basis, expect the asset to earn a return greater than x%. We can consider risk adjustment as zero in this case as the asset in question is of average risk for the company's business. If the company manufactures widgets, another machine to produce widgets would be an average risk asset for the company.

The challenges in applying net present value are determining cash flow and the required yield. These issues are outside the scope of this book.

Time frame

John Maynard Keynes (1883-1946) was a British economist whose theories became known as Keynesian Economics. He was a firm believer in government intervention both fiscally and monetarily to combat the adverse effects of economic recessions and depressions. Economists consider him one of the main founders of modern macroeconomics.[77] He is famous for saying, "In the long-run we are all dead."[78]

In this quote, Keynes countered the classical notion that government should not act when the economy is challenged by recession, boom or bust. Classic economics held that these were only short-run adjustments, but in the long-run the economy would return to stability. In times of economic woe he felt government should act through fiscal and monetary policy to lessen the pain of economic adjustment. That things would stabilize in the long-run offered no comfort as, "in the long-run we are all dead."

An economics professor once remarked in class, we may plan for the long-run, but we live in the short-run. Economics defines the long-run a point where all inputs are variable and the short-run as the point in time where one or more inputs are fixed. Inputs are labor, capital, material, *et cetera*. Long versus short does not denote a period of time, but rather how variable input is. Short and long-run will vary among industries by the nature of the production process. The production of oil is relatively fixed in the short-run because major increases in supply must entail exploration and development that can require many years to accomplish. A producer of soft drinks is only constrained by the quantity of bottles, carbon dioxide, water, sugar and distribution that can be marshaled. It operates more in the short-run as opposed to oil and gas production. All things being equal, the supply curve over time for energy will be steeper or inelastic versus the production of soft drinks. While on a relative basis one industry may be inelastic versus another, over time the tendency is for the supply curve to flatten and become more elastic as bottlenecks are overcome and new producers enter the market.

Demand can be thought of in similar terms. In the short-run the demand for gasoline to power your SUV is quite inelastic. Over time, in the long-run you could arrange to drive less, buy a more fuel efficient vehicle or buy a newfangled vehicle that is powered by nuclear fuel cells. Over time, preferences, behaviors and substitutes for products tend to flatten the demand curve. Demand, all things being equal, is more elastic in the long-term.

It would appear that in the long-run a business must be concerned with competition and obsolescence with and of its product in addition to all the things one must fret about in the short-run, where we actually live and operate.

Timing

> "Pray to the god of timing and don't screw the pooch."
>
> —The Oracle of Caddo Lake

Caddo Lake is a large natural lake in the southern U.S. covering 27,000 acres. Half the lake is in east Texas and half in northwest Louisiana. The lake was formed centuries ago by a massive logjam on the Red River called the Great Raft, located at the present day site of Shreveport, Louisiana. The first white men to discover the Raft were the Freeman-Custis Expedition sent to explore the Red River basin in 1806. They reported that the raft completely obstructed the channel of the Red River. Early in the 19th century the lake was a haven for outlaws of all types. It was noted for its racetrack, cockfights, saloons and brothels and boasted that it averaged one violent death per day. The pirate Jean Lafitte had connections to the outlaw economy. Steamboat traffic was robust in the 1830's and 1840's and was used for all types of commerce. During the American Civil War, steamers carried men and material to the rest of the Confederacy. Captain Henry Shreve, using snag boats in 1873, decimated commerce on the lake by destroying the Great Raft. Today, the lake is a beautiful preserve of nature with deer, alligators and cranes inhabiting its myriad channels.[79]

A very wealthy gentleman took me under his wing when I was in college. He liked to taunt me for my "book learning." He had made a fortune in real estate and timber and lived simply with his wife and a daughter who was a couple of years older than I was. He enjoyed talking about business, how to make money and what they were teaching me in school. He invited me on a trip down to Caddo Lake to tour it in his boat and see the sights. He had an older ski-barge with a big Evinrude outboard motor. We spent the day chatting and traveling the channels of the lake at breakneck speed. Many of the channels were only marginally wider than the boat.

We stopped for lunch and I discovered one of the reasons for his wealth. He brought a "box lunch" for us, which he produced from a crumpled paper bag. He had bologna and American cheese wrapped in wax paper with yellow mustard and half a loaf of Wonder bread. He packed each of us a cool drink of milk that was stored in a cleaned out mayonnaise jar. For dessert he had two Twinkies for each of us. They were not in the individual wrappers but rolled up in a crinkled piece of used aluminum foil. One secret to accumulating his wealth? He lived modestly as evidenced by our box lunch! It was a fine lunch, as I was very hungry and thought I might need the energy to swim out if he hit one of the many stumps we raced by. We talked about business and money and he shared *his* secret to accumulating wealth. He said the most important thing was, "pray to the god of timing and don't screw the pooch." Don't do anything stupid is simple enough to grasp, but I believe what he meant by timing is this: You may call it God's will, mojo, being in the right place at the right time, clean living or just plain luck. "Luck" is something we can't control and is a huge factor in how our plans work or don't. Without resorting to superstition, the better your endeavor comes together with ease as if it were meant to be, the more likely your stars are in line.

If you wish to insist that you create your own timing, a story from B-school comes to mind. A Business Policy class at Tulane was a wonderful experience. The professor was absolutely infatuated with L.L. Bean. This was before the Internet, so he enjoyed telling the story of his annual purchase of lined chinos from the catalog. Even though he knew his size, he would call customer service and have them get a tape to measure the rise, inseam, waist, loop width and insist they give him statistics on the thermal properties such as the weight of the fleece. Why he would need such a pant in New Orleans is beyond me, but this was an annual ritual with him that he loved to recount at any opportunity.

He posed a question in class one-day as we discussed strategy. He asked when the appropriate time for a business to change direction. One of my classmates responded, "well ahead of the turn." This classmate Charles, who we called "Charlie Tuna," was a rising executive in the shipping industry getting his MBA on the clock. He explained that they were in the tanker business and a tanker was a really big ship. It took several miles of open water to execute a turn. So, if you had to adjust course, you started well ahead of the turning point. Tuna made such a big hit with the professor that the next semester the class not only heard about L.L. Bean but about "turning the ship." The lesson in this application is that being alert at the helm improves timing.

SaLT Concepts

Time is money
Time frame matters
Pray for timing

CHAPTER 11

Product Life Cycle

The product life cycle mimics that of biological life in that a product passes through birth, growth, maturity, decline and death.[80] Companies, especially those with one product, will exhibit the same pattern. Birth, or start-up, is characterized as having a new product with low sales, high investment and negative operating cash flow. Investment takes the form of product introduction, production, marketing and market creation. Operational cash flow refers to cash flow generated from making and selling the product. Monetary investment may be high compared to working capital. Birth is painful.

Growth is characterized by sales growing at first an exponential rate and then slowing. Operational cash flow may start to turn positive, but marketing still requires investment while production efficiencies may yet be achieved. Because of growth, working capital requirements are high. This is the ravenous adolescent.

Maturity is a stabilized growth rate and a leveling of revenue. Operational cash flow is high, investment is low and working capital is minimal. Profitability should be greatest at this point as economies of scale are captured. This is the cash cow. Decline is the dwindling of the market. Production may be curtailed or consolidation may occur in the market or industry. Divestiture occurs and operational cash flow may be positive or negative, but the business should be shedding cash. If you are able to manage decline and look more like a monopoly, operating cash flow should remain healthy. If not, operational cash flow may decline with lower revenue. Death is obvious. The theory in a product and company framework is this: As your product reaches the cash cow and shedding stage, you can reinvest that money in new product development and constantly have a portfolio of products in growth, maturity and decline. In this way your company can grow at a modest yet robust clip with corresponding cash flow and increasing capitalization. The value of your company should grow at a respectable rate. When I was in Business School, the Boston Consulting Group Model (BCG Model)[81] was in vogue. It identified players as Cash Cows, Stars, Dogs and Question marks. The model was originally popularized by Bruce D. Henderson as the growth-share matrix.[82] The Cash Cows financed the Stars so they could become Cash Cows one day. The Cash Cows eventually became Dogs and were divested. There is an indeterminate category called Question Marks that could become Stars or could simply be Dogs. The Cash Cow provided the capital for the Question Marks to be identified and if warranted, fueled growth to become Stars. There exist many variations of the growth-share matrix.

Graph 11.1—Product Life Cycle, Cash Flow and Investment

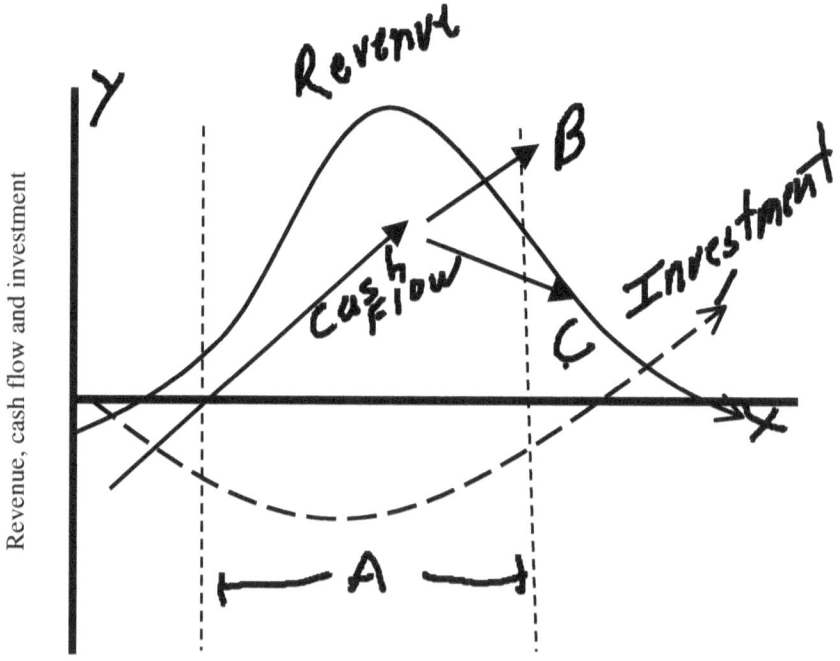

This graph depicts the relationship between life cycle, investment and cash flow. The x-axis denotes time as it passes to the right. Below the x-axis numbers are negative and positive above the axis. The y-axis details total revenue over time (top with hump being full maturity), annual operating cash flow (arrowhead) and total investment over time (concave below x-axis). The dashed vertical to the left denotes the break between start-up and growth. The dashed vertical to the right marks the break between decline and death. Between the dashed verticals are growth, maturity and decline. For our purposes we will be concerned with growth, maturity and decline as the range labeled A. As mentioned previously, operating cash flow in the decline can be stable or growing or can decline with revenue depending on the level of monopoly power achieved (Points B or C). The actual breaks will depend upon many variables including the nature of the product.

Countless marketing theories and management texts populate the notion of lengthening the growth and maturity stages. For example, lengthening can occur by the introduction of a new and improved product or a new use for the product. In 3M's case, glue and yellow paper are an example. In addition, various organizations and academicians have made further refinements of the BCG Model. These refinements of the growth-share matrix overlay market power or structure, market growth and a company's growth on top of the model to form a decision tree for strategic planning. An adaptation of the BCG Model will be illustrated in Part II, SaLT Step 3.

The point is thus: Given certain information about your business, models exist to indicate what your strategic plan should be. The SaLT method adapts these models to the small business environment. The traditional models are not formulated to meet the conditions in which a small business exists. The models gather data on large companies which are publicly traded for use in "crunching the numbers" to generate the appropriate strategic choices. Why do the models not address the small businessperson in particular? There are a number of reasons, but a very practical reason is that very little financial data exist in the public realm for individual small businesses. Publicly traded companies must file their financial data along with management's discussion of the company's results with the Securities and Exchange Commission. Academicians need data. Public filings are their source of data to carry out, among other analyses, statistical analysis.

For the small business, data is limited and not reported on an individual company basis. The Risk Management Association (RMA) publishes the *Annual Statement Studies*,[83] which combine average financial data for different classes of small business. RMA is a trade group for banking and other financial industries. They ask banks, on a confidential basis, to provide financial data for its small business customers to compile averages. Individual companies are never identified. I have participated in several submissions of data over the years. The *Statement Studies* are very useful to a lender in comparing a particular company's performance to an industry average. Another source of data for small business exists among banks in terms of expected credit losses for their small business portfolios. The Federal Reserve, through the Federal Deposit Insurance Corporation (FDIC), requires banks to reserve for expected credit losses in their small business lending portfolios. The last bit of hard data available for small business is bankruptcy filings. Experience shows that small businesses fail at higher rates than larger businesses fail. Bankruptcy filings are a way to gage the economic climate for small business. Banks use this data to predict potential credit losses for their small business portfolios. Company specific financial information in the public domain is not available.

As the models analyze large business, the small business, because of its size and market power, would generally fall into the Dog category discussed above. However if you change the frame of these models, they do give a strategic planning map for the small business. That is what the SaLT method articulates.

SaLT Concept

The SaLT method adapts strategic decision making for the small business.

CHAPTER 12

Strategy, Logistics and Tactics Overview

"However beautiful the strategy, you should occasionally look at the results."

—Attributed to Winston Churchill,
British Prime Minister during the Second World War.

The concepts of strategy, logistics and tactics are intertwined. SaLT depicts the concepts on a continuum with the ends meeting forming a circle. Strategy affects logistics and tactics just as surely as logistics and tactics affect strategy and each the other.

Strategy

"a plan of action"—strategy defined by *Oxford*.

Who are you? To develop a strategy for achieving a goal you must first be aware of who you are. What are your capabilities, strengths, weaknesses and expertise? Do you have a superior product, idea, method or process? Where are you in terms of life cycle, market position and financial position? What does your time horizon look like? As we stated in the previous chapter, you are either in growth, maturity or decline.

Who do you want to be? Let's distinguish between a Grand Strategy and an Operational Strategy. A Grand Strategy is a statement such as, "I want to be the biggest fish in the pond." An Operational Strategy is the different points you want to reach to achieve your Grand Strategy. Think of two points: Who you are and the Grand Strategy of who you want to be.

Figure 12.1—Grand and Operational Strategy

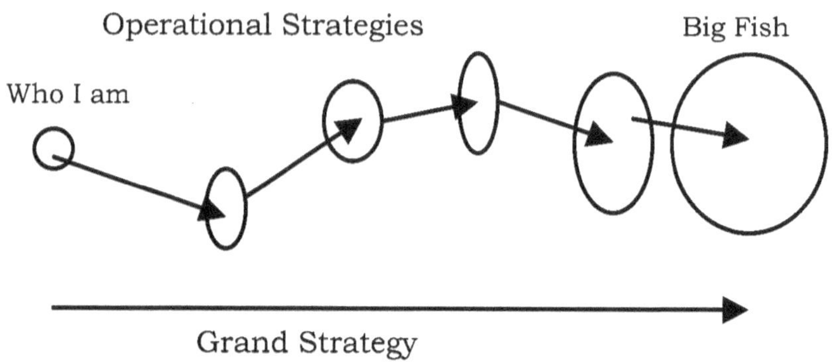

The path in achieving your Grand Strategy will most likely not be straight and direct. It will be composed of Operational Strategies with many points of adjustment. Think of dead-reckoning (determination without the aid of celestial observations, the position of a ship or aircraft from the record of the courses sailed or flown, the distance made, and the known or estimated drift) to a hilltop on the horizon with many smaller hills in between. As you begin your journey, you raise your thumb to the horizon, spotting your ultimate goal. Because of many hills between the two points, you pick a tree in the first valley to reach before darkness falls and pick another landmark to walk toward when you awake the next morning. On reaching the next hilltop, you discover your reckoning was a bit off, so you raise your thumb again, refocus on the ultimate objective and mark another spot to travel to and rest. These steps are repeated until you have reached your ultimate goal.

Who do you want to be?

A global titan; member of the S&P 500; small fish; big fish; *One fish two fish red fish blue fish?*[84]

You begin with a vision of who you want to be and compare that with who you are. Do the two make intuitive sense? Is your goal contained by your value set? Do you have the means and ability to achieve your Grand Strategy? What are the steps or Operational Strategies to achieve your Grand Strategy?

Logistics

"That things [sic] going to need clean towels and champagne brought up, there's that logistics issue there."—Jim Baker, manager of Spacehab's Apex program. Speaking of NASA's plan to retire its three remaining space shuttles by 2010. Spacehab and other private space-flight firms are hoping to win re-supply rights for the International Space Station.[85]

Logistics is having the right things in the right place at the right time. There are volumes of books, theory and views on logistics. A popular concept from my Business School days was Just-in-Time, or JIT for short. It was a logistical theory of having the things you need arrive at the moment you needed them and was widely popularized in the 1980's by Ohno Taiichi[86] at Toyota. It is a strategy to cut down on the amount of inventory carried and the cost of carrying it. It was valid in both theory and practice—and my was it popular in B-School! Professors talked of JIT this and JIT that. JIT in the morning, JIT in the evening, "ain't we got fun?"[87] Current popular logistical models include algorithms related to production planning, inventory planning and control, distribution, routing, scheduling and forecasting. Pick up any business publication and you will see the different models discussed or advertised for sale to offer you a solution. In fact, service companies exist these days that do nothing but arrange logistical solutions for your business, especially as it relates to distribution.

Tactics

"Tactics means doing what you can with what you have."—Quote generally attributed to Saul David Alinsky, (1909-1972) He is considered the father of community organizing.[88]

A colleague once distinguished tactics for me with the following example:

If you are in a street fight, and the bigger fellow hits you with his fist, do you: a.) Poke the in him in the eye? or b.) Hit him in the stomach? Tactics are the choice between a. and b. In many instances, it is difficult to distinguish between pure strategy, logistics and tactics. This is why SaLT envisions the three on a continuum with the ends joined.

A simple example of pure strategy, logistics and tactics is:

Think of planting a garden in your back yard. Your Grand Strategy is to plant a flower garden. An Operational Strategy would be to plant Mums. Logistics would be getting the flowers, the shovel and the potting soil in place to plant the garden. Tactics is determining how far apart and how deep to plant the flowers.

I have three favorite examples of strategy, logistics and tactics in the public domain of information.

Technology Example

The first example is the ongoing battle between tech firms to determine the nature of software we use. In Steve Lohr's article, "Growth Spurt; A Cyberfueled Growth Spurt," he discusses Salesforce.com and their strategy of providing solutions for the small business. Salesforce.com offers software as an online service to reach smaller companies.[89] It offers a "no-software" solution[90] and has made fantastic progress in eliminating software as we recognize it.

In my own experience, for years when preparing my taxes, I have used TurboTax's online service. With TurboTax[91] you enter your data and it spits out your tax return for filing. TurboTax offers two alternatives. The first is the traditional way of buying the software and loading it on your home computer. The second way is interacting with their website to enter your information and then printing the resulting tax return on your printer at home. You buy the use of their website as a service. TurboTax also stores your tax return for future access. The fee you pay resembles a subscription. I use the software-free method. The beauty of this method is that I don't have to fiddle with software on my home computer or worry about upgrades and storing the information. My computer could "crash" at any time destroying my data. The battle now rages among the tech companies like Salesforce.com that would make software loaded on your home computer obsolete. This is a fine example of a Grand Strategy.

Alaskan Pipeline

An example of logistics and tactics, especially logistics, is the construction of the Alaskan Pipeline in the 1970's. Set aside for a moment your feelings about wilderness versus drilling policy. I make no judgments on these values. It can be said that the construction of the pipeline was a logistical triumph. Huge oil reserves had been discovered on the North Slope of Alaska in the late 1960's, but the conundrum was how to move it. The seas were usually frozen, so transportation by ship was made nearly impossible. Many alternatives were considered, including flying the oil in huge air tankers.[92] The best alternative found was to build a pipeline from the North Slope to Valdez, the most northern ice-free port available. The following facts are compiled from the Alyeska Pipeline Website:

> The pipeline is 800 miles long with a diameter of 48 inches. It crosses three mountain ranges and 800 rivers and streams. Construction commenced on March 27, 1975 and was completed on June 20, 1977 at a cost in 1977 dollars of $8 Billion. The pipeline has carried 14 billion barrels of oil since its completion. Construction materials shipped to Alaska carried a total weight of 3 million tons. 108,000 welds of pipe were completed to build it. At the peak, 28,000 people were employed in 30 construction camps along the pipeline.[93]

While the pipeline was 800 miles long, the work area occupied only 12 square miles of land area.[94] Public Broadcasting produced and aired an *American Experience* documentary on the pipeline. It documented through interviews and television footage the immensity of the project, controversies surrounding it, and the story of construction told be the people who worked on or were involved with the project. A transcript of that broadcast was obtained from the website, and the following information is part of that transcript.

> Federal legislation finally paved the way for construction to begin in the face of tremendous opposition. The controversies surrounding the project include, permafrost, migratory animals, court battles initiated by environmentalists and falsification of documentation on weld integrity. An item in the documentary that peaked my interest was the role played by Pipeline Welders Union Local 798 from Tulsa, Oklahoma.[95] Local 798 had skills developed in North Sea projects that no one else had. They perfected welding thick pipe similar to the thickness planned for the Alaskan Pipeline. Because of this skill, Local 798 was given the lead welding role on the project. The narrator made the point that, "[Local 798] were the highest paid and most demanding workers on the job." Jimmy Pedigo, a welder, stated, "... I know there was a saying up there that happiness was an Okie flying south with a Texan under each arm." He was

remarking on the fact that the welders were considered "primma donnas." Whatever the reputation, Local 798 was instrumental in completing the project. The project manager, Frank Moolin, was also instrumental in the project working tirelessly to finish the project on time. The documentary comments that Moolin, a relatively young man in his early forties, died a few years after the project was completed. The implication being that the enormity of the project caused an early death. With an original budget of approximately $1 billion, overruns occurred due to conditions and the desire to have the project finished on time. Oil revenue lost was estimated at $22 million per day that pipeline completion was delayed. Bill Fowler, assistant project manager, articulated the stakes this way, "I've hired aircraft, spent $10,000 to go get a $50 item for a Caterpillar tractor to get it started so we can keep it moving." He goes on to remark, "You know, it doesn't matter what it takes to get the widget; go get the widget."[96]

The $50 widget that cost $10,050 is the apogee of the logistical dilemma. Frank Moolin was voted Man of the year by *Engineering News-Record* in 1976. According to the February 19th, 1976 *ENR* article on Moolin, he was a 1956 graduate of the University of Illinois and was saddled with a reputation as a loner with a ruthless talent for the project management. He had worked as a lead on BART, the Bay Area Rapid Transit system around San Francisco, as well as other projects in the Far East. The press nicknamed him "the barracuda."[97] The original budget for the pipeline was $1 Billion and cost $8 Billion to complete. This is a huge cost overrun. It shows one way out of a logistical dilemma: You spend your way out. In today's dollars if one applies the consumer price index to the completion date in 1977, the amount spent on the project (CPI 1977—2005)[98] is $26 Billion. As the pipeline is estimated to have carried 14 Billion barrels of oil to date,[99] at an average of $30 per barrel, the revenue generated is $420 Billion. The cost overrun seems insignificant in comparison.

Southwest Airlines

Southwest Airlines is an example of effective integration of strategy, logistics and tactics. It is extremely popular in my region of the U.S. and is considered the pioneer of the low cost, no frills airline. The airline and its stock are often portrayed by the media as a Wall Street darling. I analyzed the airline and presented my conclusions to a Business Policy class at the

University of Tulsa about a decade ago. Since then, I have been a loyal customer and have been awed by the service and low fares the airline offers. Given a choice among airlines, I always fly Southwest. The class did not like my conclusions as to the reasons for Southwest's success. The students weighed very heavily the fact that Southwest was superior because they saved money on food service and had really happy employees. I countered that the success stemmed from the fact they had full passenger loads that I supported with data from Southwest's annual reports. I theorized their success was attributable to full loads as:

1. They occupied a niche in the market of low fares with good service.

2. While service was limited in the region at the time, the point-to-point versus spoke-hub system allowed for simplification of logistics and cherry picking of routes. Unlike American Airlines, they don't have to fly everywhere to make their model work.

3. Motivated employees were critical to the model.

4. Lack of food service was a function of short point-to-point flights. A flight of one hour or less does not allow for food service. Food cost in and of itself did not matter as the food cost was relatively nominal. However, not serving food was a big logistical factor in short gate turnaround time.

5. As aircraft and it infrastructure are expensive, having the aircraft flying with paying customers versus sitting on the tarmac waiting to be loaded with food and customers was counterintuitive to the students' argument attributing success to low food cost and happy employees.

As I reviewed my notes from that presentation in the writing of this book, I still feel my conclusions remain valid. If you look at the price of the stock and the annualized returns, you find the following: Since 1980, Southwest has posted a 19% annual increase in share price consistently out performing the market as a whole and the transportation index in particular over the review period.[100] It has 32 straight years of profitability and is the only airline to remain profitable since the challenges of 9/11/2001.[101]

The Southwest Airlines Website details the following information.

> The idea began on a cocktail napkin 30 years ago with the first routes between Dallas, Houston and San Antonio. It is not unusual to see a Vice President pitch in to assist gate staff in loading the aircraft. Southwest employs 31,000 people who

strive to have fun on the job. Employees routinely dress-up and decorate gates for holidays, tell silly jokes and sing in-flight instructions to passengers. It follows a strategy of using the same airplane for all flights: A Boeing 737. All seating is first class, its only class. Southwest will enter a new market only when the market will support a threshold number flights a day. It doesn't offer seat assignments [at this writing] and prides itself on quick gate turnaround.[102]

Southwest specifically endeavors to keep its planes full:

1. They enter a new market when the market will support a threshold number of flights a day. They don't claim to fly to every market. They cherry pick.

2. They fly only one aircraft type: A Boeing 737. Maintenance logistics and costs, pilot profile and training, flight attendant logistics, and overall logistics are the same with all flights.

3. When a fight arrives it is immediately loaded and put back in the air. They don't fiddle with seat assignments, and ensure a quick off-load and cabin prep for the next flight. Flight changes by passengers or special needs aren't considered a big deal. Things are kept simple. Once in the air, you are quickly given a beverage of your choice. Even alcohol is treated without hassle.

Keep it simple! Southwest, as part of its frequent flyer program, gives out free drink coupons. When flying, I carry a stack of them and no one around me pays for a drink. I have more than I can even give away! How does this help Southwest? They don't have to struggle with making change for a passenger wanting a beer. Flight attendants hate dealing with cash and making change. They have told me so. It is rare to see a Southwest attendant counting bills. What would they do with cash collected anyway? What are the logistics and controls of collection and dispatch? Given that a 737 holds on average 150 passengers,[103] if half the passengers want a drink and the cost to the Southwest is $2 per drink, it equates to $150 dollars. This is a nominal amount of money considering fare, fuel and crew. The flight attendants and the passengers are happy. Southwest is happy as they don't have to waste time with what to do with the cash, nor do they have to fret about the attendant needing change or the controls to capture fraud.

Another example of simplicity is flight coupons earned by the frequent flier. Southwest awards a coupon after 8 round trips. The coupon can be used anywhere, at anytime for any fare subject to the same availability as the paying customer. How much money does Southwest save in administration using this simple approach versus other airlines who seem to go out of their way to keep you from using your miles? How much happier are Southwest's customers? Sounds like a win-win. These are trivial examples of efficiency, but it punctuates how Southwest translates simplicity into efficiency and warm feelings from its work force and passengers.

Flying with other carriers reminds me of a scene from *Monty Python's The Meaning of Life* when the Headmaster is explaining the day's activities to the class.

> Now before I begin the lesson will those of you who are playing in the match this afternoon move your clothes down on to the lower peg immediately after lunch before you write your letter home, if you're not getting your hair cut, unless you've got a younger brother who is going out this weekend as the guest of another boy, in which case collect his note before lunch, put it in your letter after you've had your hair cut, and make sure he moves your clothes down onto the lower peg for you.[104]

The full story of Southwest is longer and more complicated than described in this book. In general, Southwest is a niche airline that through its strategy, logistics and tactics strives for efficiency and full air-craft. By almost any measure, Southwest has been a success for its customers, employees and shareholders. The challenge for Southwest is to preserve their niche as they continue growing. As they look more like American Airlines, the law of diminishing returns will set in causing it to be more difficult to retain its niche.

SaLT Concept

Strategy, logistics and tactics are difficult to separate and can be best ana-lyzed on the continuum.

CHAPTER 13

SaLT and the Fishing Analogy

"You can't catch a fish if you don't have your hook in the water."
—Alton, a very wise southern fisherman

Early one morning as I was drafting the chapter on Guns and Butter, my nine year-old stepson, Tyler, wandered into my office, a stuffed bear under his arm, cheeks puffy from slumber and inquired as to what I was doing. I explained I was writing a book for the small businessperson and talking about guns and butter. With a look of utter confusion he said, "guns and butter? Guns and butter? Those don't have anything to do with each other. Blake, one is a gun, the other is butter." He turned and left the room shaking his head as if to imply I was an idiot. You may ask what do SaLT and fishing have to do with each other? By the end of this chapter it will be crystal clear.

I grew up learning how to fish in the southern United States: the South, proper. We fish for certain species in a certain way, which I will describe. I'm not sure what they do up north, say in Missouri. I have seen on television how they fish up near the Arctic Circle in Minnesota. They have fish they call Pike and Walleye. They even fish in the winter through the ice. They have shacks they pull out on a frozen lake, drill a hole and fish through the ice. They use funny looking shorty poles, and on television the men have parkas on and talk about how wonderful nature is and how ice fishing is a tradition. I never really understood the concept of ice fishing until I was married. Before you were married, if you wanted to get together with your friends and tell tales, tall and true, you just joined the gang at the bar.

Saltwater fishing, as opposed to analyzing fishing in terms of SaLT, will not be discussed as I am not addressing the global titans in the world, just as I will not discuss the saltwater sport-fisherman, trawler or long-liner. To begin our analysis we need to define some terms:

Strategy is the species and body of water to be fished. I haven't included Crappie fishing as it can cross strategies and confuse the reader.

Brim—Technically known as a Bluegill with the scientific name *Lepomis macrochirus*. It is about the size of one's open hand and can be caught larger or smaller in size, but "hand-sized" is a respectable specimen. They are usually near the bank and like docks, brush and other underwater infrastructure. They love crickets and congregate in nests. In general, if you haven't caught one in 30 seconds, they either aren't biting or they aren't there so you move on to the next likely spot. Once biting, they tend to frenzy and can be caught on a bare hook. Brimming is a lot of fun and well suited for the younger fisherman. It takes quite a few to make a mess, but it doesn't take long. They are usually fished for in a pond from the bank or in a Johnboat.

Bass—This is the large-mouth bass or *Micropterus salmoides*. The large-mouth bass is easily recognizable by its large, gaping mouth when open. It is a predator fish that feeds on minnows or very small Brim. The world record was caught June 2, 1932 by 20-year-old George Perry near Jacksonville, Georgia and weighed 22 pounds, 4 ounces. It was caught on an oxbow lake off the Ocmulgee River.[105] The fish was approximately 32 inches in length. On a really good outing, a 10-pounder would be cause for celebration, and your wife would forgive your misdeeds for a 6-pounder. 1 to 3 pounds is average. These are considered big game hunting in the South. You catch very few, if any, and they are found in larger ponds and lakes. A pole will work, but more commonly a rod is used. A Johnboat with a motor or a Bass Boat is used as your platform and you fish in coves off the main channel of the lake where the underwater infrastructure includes logs, stumps and submerged brush.

Catfish—It is known as a Channel Catfish or *Ictalurus punctatus*. Catfishing has many variations in the South, but I am a jug-man through and through. Jug fishing entails an overnight trip to the river with a Johnboat and a dozen or so empty bleach jugs. You tie a length of line to the jug and bait it with chicken liver. You set the jugs out at dusk from your Johnboat to the right and left of the channel where the river turns and the water collects in a pool. You don't set in fast water unless you want to chase jugs. At midnight you collect your catch or re-bait and haul in again after breakfast. You usually catch plenty of 2 and 3 pound fish, more than enough for a mess to fry at the bank of the river. It is a venue where many tales, tall and true are told and retold.

Pond—These are delineated by the terms large and small. They are usually round or oval in shape with the small type giving access to all points along the "bank" or water's edge. A small pond usually is defined as one that you can throw a rock across to the opposing bank. The rock would be about the size of a golf ball. A large pond gives bank access and is big enough for a Johnboat, but not so large that a motor is required. Small ponds are perfect habitats for Brim and smaller Bass. They are well suited for the younger fisherman. A large pond needs a Johnboat with a paddle for access to all habitats. If you were set on mechanization you could mount a trolling motor, but usually a paddle is all that is needed so you can access the nooks and crannies offering the best habitat. When I was a youngster, my family lived on a large pond. However, I felt it was more ocean-like. I was convinced some great battle of the American Civil War was fought on its banks. It was idyllic for a young boy who loved to fish. The "lake" as I called it had many stumps and fallen trees and offered exceptional Brimming. Many larger Bass up to the 5-pound mark populated the "lake," and numerous happy hours were spent in the family Johnboat.

On one occasion, extended family came for a spell or visit, including my grandfather affectionately known as Pap. Pap, my aunt's husband Roy and I went fishing one afternoon as it threatened rain. We did pretty well until the storm began. As we paddled in toward the bank, we high-centered on a stump and the boat started rotating in a circular fashion as Pap in the back and Roy at the front paddled in opposing directions. I learned several things that afternoon. Being a regular Sunday School attendee, I thought Jesus Christ was that fellow in the painting at the church. Much to my surprise Roy had transfigured into J.C. As we rotated on the stump, Pap kept looking at the sky hollering, "Jesus, what are you doing?" Roy would look back and answer tersely, "paddling."

When we returned to the house, my father asked what had happened to us out there and Pap said, "he and Roy weren't geeing and hawing." Since tensions were high at the time, I didn't inquire as to Pap's meaning. I thought it had something to do with J.C. Roy geed when he should have hawed. It wasn't until years later that I discovered what gee and haw meant. Gee is what you shout at a mule to cause it to turn right. Haw is shouted to cause the mule to turn left.

Lake—These come in large and small. They are usually the result of damming a river and the small variety is easily accessible to a Johnboat with a 10 h.p. motor mounted on the back. Evinrude is the preferred outboard. A smaller Bass boat such as a Bass Tracker with 50 horses or less is also well suited. A full sized Bass boat on a small lake is overkill and a breach of etiquette as they make big waves that rock the smaller boats. On your Johnboat you could put a bigger motor on it such as a 25 h.p., but then you need a stout fellow to sit in the front to hold the bow in the water. This arrangement can become unstable when conditions are windy or if a storm were to form.

On a large lake the full sized Bass boat is needed, as you will be traveling some distance to find the right habitat. These are the boats that you see on television in Bass fishing tournaments. They are big, new, shiny and have 125 h.p. minimum. You also need a large, new, expensive pickup truck for towing with paint that usually matches the boat's color. Our analysis will ignore large lakes. Why spend all that money and travel over that much water when a small lake would meet your needs to fish?

River—These are not characterized by the Arkansas or Mississippi but have names such as Cossatot and Illinois. The general rule follows that of pond size. If you can't throw a rock to the opposing bank, the river is too big.

Logistics will cover the type of boat or fishing platform, its transport, tackle and bait needed.

The Bank—You stand on the bank to fish from the edge of the water. It is ideal placement for small ponds and well suited for large ones.

Johnboat—It is a flat-bottomed aluminum boat 12-feet long and 2-feet deep. It has a small seat in the front, a bench in the middle and a bench in the back. A grown man can generally stretch his arms perpendicular to his body and grab the sides of the Johnboat. It has two gunwales for oars in the center of the boat used to tie your fish stringer. You don't use oars but each bench has a paddle like you would in a canoe. You may ask, "why not a canoe?" My answer is stability. The 12-footer has plenty of room for two adults and two kids. It also fits in the back of your GOB for transport.

A GOB is a "good ol' boy" pickup truck. Usually it is an older model Chevrolet with or without a boat rack. The boat rack is redundant, as a 12-footer will fit into the back of the GOB with the gate down. It is very common for the GOB to have faded paint, dents, scratches and rusted side-panels. A sure sign of a GOB is that it leaves a trail of black fumes belching such when first started. It may also have holes in the muffler giving it a distinct sound making nighttime identification reliable.

Bass boat or Tracker—This is not the "professional" model discussed above, but basically a Johnboat on steroids. It is a bit longer, wider and taller. It has a deck that you stand on instead of a bottom with storage between the two. It has the high mounted swivel chairs for casting, trolling motor, a fish finder, depth finder, steering wheel, and is towed on a trailer. It is perfectly acceptable to use your GOB for towing. You don't waste time Brimming with this. It is a Bass boat.

Pole—Usually cane, but synthetic varieties are available. It is 10-to-12 feet long with an equal length of fishing line. Your effective reach is approximately 15 feet. It has a bobber, lead shot weight and a hook. Once baited, you swing and drop your bait into a preferred spot. When the bobber sinks you pull. It is ideal for Brim and small Bass.

Rod—Meaning a rod/reel combo. This refers to a rod for casting the line, and a reel to wind the line onto the spool. There are 3 basic types of reels with corresponding rods. A casting reel has an open spool and is used for distance to place the lure in the correct spot. A strong cast often results in a "bird nest" or tangled spool. The spinning reel has an open spool with a half-moon guide. It is used less for distance but more for placement. It is ideal for jigging. The spin casting reel has a covered spool with a trigger for line release. It is well suited for distance, placement and ease of use with Zebco being a desirable brand. Models 202 and 404[106] are extremely popular. For kids, they offer a "Snoopy" model for skill development so they can eventually upgrade to a 202. These are light and medium reels ideal for the southern fisherman.

Crickets—Live bait you buy by the tube and they come in different sizes. The cheapest is usually my preference. Crickets and minnows are purchased at the Bait Shop. The Bait Shop will also carry the obligatory potted meat, Vienna sausage, sardines, soda crackers, Moon Pies and whatever kind of coke you want. Coke means Coca-Cola, Dr. Pepper, 7-UP or Root Beer. I'm not sure that I ever saw a Pepsi in a Bait Shop in my heyday.

Minnow—Live bait purchased by the dozen. You need a minnow bucket. They come in different sizes but again, the cheapest works just fine. If you want really big bait for the monster Bass, catch a small Brim on a cricket.

Lure—Also known as artificial bait. Worms, spoons, spinners, jigs and top-water are examples. I'm a top-water man and prefer the Rapala. The top-water looks like a minnow with treble hooks on the bottom. The bait wiggles like a struggling minnow as it is reeled in. My personal favorite is the Rapala Original Floater.[107] I don't really care for anything else.

Hooks, line, bobbers and weights can be purchased at the Bait Shop and are stored in your tackle box. It is an 18"x8"x8" box with fold out trays and a handle.

Tactics concerns placement of bait in an appropriate habitat.

Poling—Dropping the baited hook in a desired spot and wait for the bobber to jiggle. You move the bait quickly if Brimming, slowly if Bass fishing.

Casting—It is for lure placement in the desired spot. You cast then retrieve with the action depending upon the lure.

Jugging—Used for Catfish. You need plastic jugs, line, hook and bait is usually chicken liver. You throw the jug into water at an appropriate spot for later collection.

Grand Strategy—To catch a "mess" of fish. A "mess" is an amount of fish to fry to feed the fishing party.

Table 13.1—Operational Strategy

X = ideal 0 = OK	Pond	Big pond or small lake	Lake	River
Brim	X	0		
Bass	0	X	X	
Catfish				X

From our table above, choices are limited depending upon the body of water. If we choose only the best strategies for each body of water, we can SaLT our choices.

Table 13.2—SaLT of Choices Available

	Pond	Big pond or small lake	Lake	River
Species of fish	Brim	Bass or Brim	Bass	Catfish
Boat	None	Johnboat, motor optional	Bass	John
Transport	None	GOB	GOB	GOB
Rod	Pole	Pole or Spincast	Spincast	Jug
Bait	Cricket	Live or Lure	Lure	Liver
Tactic	Poling	Poling or Casting	Casting	Jugging

SaLT for the small pond, lake and river is crystal clear. We need to do a bit more analysis on the big pond/small lake option. Given what we know about fishing in the South, let's distinguish between the two:

If it is truly a big pond, then we don't need a motor on the Johnboat. We will be paddling around the pond. A pole might better serve us as we can easily and quietly move into position. Because the tackle is very inexpensive, we could bring two poles, one for Brim and one for Bass with both crickets and minnows as bait. This way we could adapt to actual conditions as they present themselves.

If it is truly a small lake then we will need a motor to get around which means we need some distance between the boat and the bait-placement point. Casting seems in order for exclusively Bass.

We have five distinct SaLT Circles. Our only task is to determine the nature and size of our big pond or small lake.

SaLT Concept

In fishing, it's just noodles! This holds true for any task if you break a complicated activity into its component parts and analyze according to the choices available. For fishing, the five choices or SaLT Circles are:

1. Poling for Brim from the bank
2. Johnboating for Brim or Bass
3. Johnboating for Bass
4. Bass fishing
5. Jugging for Cats

CHAPTER 13.1

SaLT and Fishing
It's Just Noodles!
Right?

Is it just noodles? Yes, in some ways it is, and in some ways it's not. Let's remember the following **SaLT Concepts:**

1. *Ceteris Paribus*
2. Be aware of the assumptions
3. Avoid loss of perspective
4. Have a simple plan
5. Too much information can lead to inaction
6. Ignorance doesn't lead to an optimal outcome
7. Framing matters

If you don't know anything about fishing, especially fresh water sport fishing in North America, you might think that I know quite a lot about it. Through the SaLT method, I gave you five SaLT circles that would lead to a successful fishing trip. I made a number of assumptions, changed the perspective of the analysis and gave a simple plan for mastery. I limited the overall amount of information, but made you an expert in fishing as I framed it.

If I applied the five SaLT Circles to Minnesota, Missouri, the brackish waters of the Chesapeake Bay or marshes of Florida, Louisiana or Texas, I might look silly. If I applied the five SaLT Circles to trout fishing in the Rocky Mountains, might my fellow fishermen laugh at me? How ludicrous would I look dragging my Johnboat across the ice in Minnesota? Would the ice-fishermen take me in the shack and dunk my head through the ice-hole to sober me? I also excluded salt-water fishing from the analysis. On a long-liner, they might use me as bait and my Johnboat as a float for the line. In this way, it isn't just noodles. Fishing overall is more complex.

In a way, it is just noodles. If I didn't make assumptions, frame my assumptions, understand who I am, where I wanted to go or how I would get there, I couldn't say much about fishing. I could only say this with confidence: Fish exist, and they live in water. There are methods for removing them from the water. Once out of the water and secured, I might make a meal of them. Now that's not very helpful.

Remembering my five SaLT Circles for fishing, let's illustrate how strategy, logistics and tactics must form a continuum with the ends connected. Years ago, I dated a very nice girl. Debbie's father asked me to go Bass fishing with him one Saturday. We were in the South, proper. We had a big Bass boat, rods and tackle; everything we needed to catch fish on a very big lake. I assumed that we would find an enticing cove and fish a beautiful stretch near the bank where logs, trees and other underwater infrastructures existed.

We arrived in our big pick-up with our matching boat. We launched the boat and tore across the lake. We get to the middle of the lake, and Debbie's father stops the boat and turns off the motor. We are hundreds of yards from shore. I thought the man might have had too much coffee that morning and since no other boats were in sight, he was going to relieve himself. As I waited for the sound of water hitting water, he whipped out his rod and started casting into the middle of the lake. He looked at me noticing that I had a surprised look on my face and said, "I heard the big fish are in deeper water today." I didn't have the heart to tell him they meant five feet of water instead of two feet, and they certainly didn't mean two hundred feet of depth. Needless to say we didn't catch any fish that day. All was perfect, but our tactics failed. We didn't even have a chance of success.

SaLT Concept

Strive for simplicity and unity as you analyze and execute options.

CHAPTER 14

SaLT Illustration
Blue Boy
Logistical or Tactical Failure?

Several years ago, my extended family wanted to attend a Dallas Cowboy football came on Thanksgiving Day. As we usually watched the game on television during our celebration, it seemed a natural extension to actually attend. Having arrived at Texas Stadium a bit before the game, we took advantage of our VIP pass to go the beer tent. Inside a band was playing. I assume it was a local band sponsored by one of the beer labels. As the lead singer crooned, he had a group of dancers wearing very short cheerleader skirts. Mothers covered young boy's eyes as the dancers swished, swayed and gave an unavoidable view of flesh with an alluring flick of the skirt. In the stadium, there was a fireworks display for the pre-game show, and mini-blimps advertising soft drinks whirred overhead. The Salvation Army Red Kettle Christmas Kickoff Half-Time Gala featured singers Randy Travis and Linda Davis.[108] Unfortunately, Dallas lost to Minnesota that day with a final score of 46 to 36.[109] Even though Dallas lost, it remained a real Texas hoopla.

Texas Stadium's seating is arranged in an oval around the field with seating from the goal line around the endzone being rather distant from the action. Our seats were not endzone proper, but rather cattycornered. The game could be better viewed on the big screens situated around the stadium. There was a fellow sitting immediately behind us in his early twenties whose apparent goal was to do a "HI MOM" on television. He had painted himself Cowboy Blue from the waist up including his face and hair. He had a big "HI MOM" sign, pompoms and a whistle. He was prepared. I will add that paint is a bit of a misnomer. It was more of a dye. Having unintentionally bumped into him several times, the dye never came off onto me. It was also impervious to sweat and didn't run or streak.

As the game began, his enthusiasm for his endeavor was unbridled. He jumped up and down, waved his sign, blew his whistle, shook his pom-poms and shouted, "Go Cowboys." No matter how hard he tried he couldn't get a camera to pan him. He continued until the beginning of the fourth quarter when he collapsed head in hands, obviously exhausted from his efforts. Those of us sitting around him were not only tired for him, but were also tired of him. It was our first chance to enjoy the game in relative peace. An older Texan sitting behind leaned forward and said loudly enough for all to hear, "Hell son, I guess you just ain't blue enough."

While the Texan's comment was quite funny, I thought he missed the point. Blue Boy was blue enough. He had a breakdown of either logistics or tactics. Let's apply a SaLT analysis to Blue Boy.

Strategy—Have a "HI MOM" moment on television.

Blue boy knew who he was: a football fan. He clearly knew what he wanted to accomplish. It fit his value set; it could be reasonably accomplished. Success had a high utility value. Failure carried minimal risk of losing capital, self-respect and effort. His strategy seemed sound.

Logistics—get tickets; paint self blue; get pompoms; make sign; get to game on time.

He accomplished every item on his list. He had the ingredients. Was he in the right place at the right time? One could argue he was not in the right place to maximize his chance of success. The cattycornered seats in the endzone were not where the cameras were located, nor were they likely to pan no matter how blue he was. He could have bought seats nearer the field on the 50-yard line and had a better chance to "HI MOM" given camera placement.

Did Blue boy recognize this error before hand? If he did not recognize this, I would say he had a tactical failure. If he did realize it, perhaps the better seats were priced out of his means. This would be a logistical failure. In the first instance, the best tactic would have been to be well placed for the cameras. In the second instance, realizing the tactical value, he simply didn't have the resources.

Tactics—be in the right place; jump up and down; make noise; draw attention. Given our discussion of logistics, his tactics seem perfectly sound. Indeed, I think either way the placement issue occurred, once in place and realizing he was not properly placed, he double-downed on jumping, *et cetera*.

In this way we can applaud the flexibility inherent in his plan in meeting unexpected challenges. Even with perfect placement, he was not assured of a "HI MOM." Chance played a factor, which he could not control. However he wasn't perfectly placed. If he simply didn't have enough resources and satisficed the situation, his efforts as a whole can be judged positively in terms of SaLT.

Figure 14.1—Blue Boy's SaLT

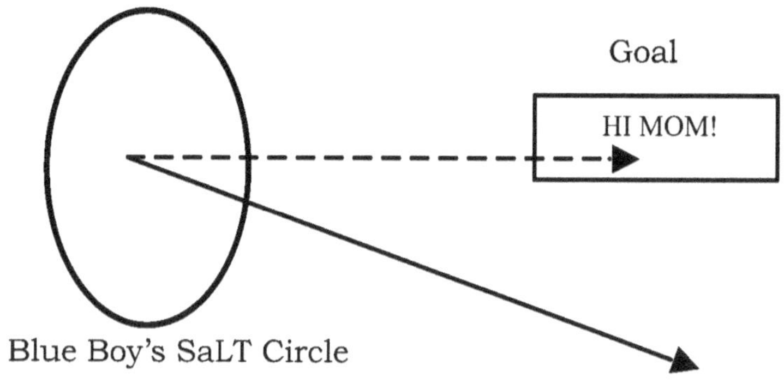

Goal

HI MOM!

Blue Boy's SaLT Circle

SaLT Concept

In Blue Boy's case, his SaLT Circle was valid because he satisficed. However, his placement for the camera was not perfect. His expected path, the solid arrow, did not get Blue Boy to his moment. He needed luck to intervene on his behalf. With a great deal of luck, his path could have been the dashed arrow.

CHAPTER 15

SaLT Illustration
Tulsa Sound
Did SaLT Dissolve?

In 1990, as a newly minted MBA and employed, I wanted a high-end Audio/Video setup. As an audiophile wannabee, I was not aware of the ante to purchase this type product. Oklahoma Records was hands down the provider of high-end product in our area. A system was custom designed for the customer and equipment specially ordered by Oklahoma Records. Oklahoma Records did not have an inventory on hand, but sold its preferred components from demos. They managed the delivery, technical requirements and installation of the equipment. In 1990, Circuit City and Best Buy had not infiltrated our market, so a continuum of product was not readily available. In that year Oklahoma Records was at the apogee of its business model with Best Buy and Circuit City on the horizon, but barely visible enough to capture notice.

I suppose that I just didn't look the part of someone that would actually make a purchase. I was given only cursory attention for a few minutes until a "real" customer walked in who was given the VIP treatment, which included a cold drink and personal attention of the owner. The store was tastefully decorated with nice carpet and fashionably edgy furniture and paints. They had a soundproof room where you could have your hair blown back sampling their product. Realizing that I was out of my league, I left feeling chagrined, making a much lower-end purchase elsewhere.

In 2001, with Oklahoma Records' business at a low tide and the owner desiring retirement, he closed the shop, which sat vacant with the sign still adorning the front. About six months later I happened to drive by and witnessed remodeling activity. I made some inquiries and found that a young fellow had bought the customer list and subleased the space from the former owner who still had a couple of years left on the lease. In about a month, Tulsa Sound was open for business.

At about the same time, Suburban Audio opened for business in a brand new shopping center in our market. It was an extremely handsome storefront working on the same model as Oklahoma Records, although it had an updated look and new generation of preferred product. I decided to pop in for a visit thinking the time had come to upgrade my system. Since I was a little older and seemingly more affluent, I was at least given attention from the staff. As I priced the different components, I saw names such as Rotel, LG, Marantz, Bowers & Wilkins, Crestron, Lutron and others. This time, I was given a seat in the soundproof room and yes, my hair was blown back. We discussed my needs and sat down with a cold drink and discussed price. $1,500 for a receiver, $20,000 for Bowers & Wilkins loud speaker set (they were really nice), $5,000 for a player, $15,000 for a television (flat screen plasma of course) and $5,000 for surround. Quick addition gave $46,500 for the components alone. Then we discussed installation for the entire house and furniture options for the home theater. Suburban Audio did say that top-end speaker wire was thrown in for free! I took the manager's card, said I would get back to them and left as quickly as I could. The ante exceeded my desire to play.

Out of curiosity I surveyed Tulsa Sound's offering. They had only been open for a month or so. As I drove up, I noticed that Oklahoma Records' sign was still on the marquee out front even though the business had changed hands and names. The décor was rather Spartan, but clean with a couple of mid-range demo units and bare walls. The only employee around was an installation guy who was having lunch from the Gyros joint a couple of doors down. We chatted for a few minutes about the store. He told me that the owner had a full time job but his wife was usually here in the mornings before the kids got out of school. I asked about the owner's background in A/V and was told that he had a really cool system at home that he had wired himself. I asked what kind of components, and he indicated JVC and Philips. Tulsa Sound would special order the stereo, deliver and hook up the equipment and run wire if they could get into my attic. I thanked the employee and left. On my way out the parking lot, I noticed that this very upscale shopping center from 12 years ago had not fared well in the intervening years. The nature of the tenants had also changed. 12 years ago Oklahoma Records was flanked by a bookstore and a Kinko's. The Gyros shop I mentioned and a Tan-N-Nail flanked Tulsa Sound. A few weeks later I passed by the store and noticed a new sign for Tulsa Sound. It was a vinyl overlay on the old marquee that in many ways didn't make one think high-end.

Let's examine Tulsa Sound's SaLT:

Strategy

The new owner wanted to take over Oklahoma Records' business and transform it into a viable enterprise for his family. This is a reasonable enough desire.

Who was the new owner? He was someone who held full time employment outside the business and arguably didn't have a wealth of expertise in A/V.

Who did the New Owner want to be? Best Buy? Circuit City? Suburban Audio? If you were to quiz Tulsa Sound's owner, he would tell you he wanted to be like Suburban Audio for the mid to low-end product. Does a low volume, high value added niche exist for the middle and low-end? You can't do volume and offer pricing and you don't have the expertise or ambiance for the higher profit high-end. Analyzing logistics and tactics is difficult, as the strategy is not apparently reasonable in this case. To compete with Suburban Audio, a different level of expertise, product offering and ambiance would be needed. To compete directly with Best Buy and Circuit City, a level of inventory would need to be on hand with sufficient scale to capture pricing discounts from suppliers. Volume for this strategy would also need to be higher than facilities permitted. Did Tulsa Sound have the wherewithal both from a capital and/or expertise point of view to place themselves in a competitive position with either Best Buy or Suburban Audio? This strategy leads you to believe the best alternative would be to define Tulsa Sound as an installer and for it to become a preferred vendor for the chains. Indeed, within 12 months Tulsa Sound closed its doors. In Tulsa Sound's case, the strategy was not reasonable.

Figure 15.1—Tulsa Sound's SaLT Circle

SaLT Concept

Tulsa Sound's Salt Circle never closed to form an unbroken continuum. The strategy was flawed to an extent that no level of logistics or tactics could overcome it.

PART II

Practice

As discussed previously, Part I covered theory. Part II covers SaLT in practice in the real world. In Part I, a number of theories were covered with appropriate academic citation to people who created the theories. In Part II, I will rely on my real-world experience in dealing with scores of small businesses. Part II is organized as SaLT Method Steps. Because of the wide variety of industries, products and services covered, I must rely on composite sketches. As in the previous Part, I must also protect the privacy of my clients and local businesses. In previous chapters, especially the Fishing Chapter, I made liberal use of assumptions and generalities. This was intentional. A blob cannot be analyzed. All that one can say about a blob is that it is a blob.

Blob, "a small roundish mass"—*The Oxford American Dictionary.*

SaLT in Practice
Step 1

Definitions and Delineation

I will better describe the small business that is the target of this book.

Small Business Owner—We will shorten this to SBO—It is the owner of the small business, usually the founder.

Product—This is what you sell. In this frame, it is considered a more standard product. It could be retail or wholesale.

Widget—This is a specialized version of the product. A made-to-order pizza versus a frozen pizza purchased at the store.

Service—This is defined as customer service or value added in terms of expertise, know-how or knowing where to get it. Using the pizza analogy, you know all the pizza places, can help the customer chose the type of pizza he/she wants, and assist in the special order and delivery.

Product-Widget-Service Circle (PWS)—On the continuum, as a SBO, you provide all aspects of PWS. One aspect may be more heavily weighted than the others are by the nature of the business, but the value you add to your customer is related to all three aspects. Product-widget-service on the continuum and joined at the ends is the PWS Circle. It is a very similar concept to SaLT that has been discussed, except instead of addressing who-how-where you want to be, we are addressing the value you add to your ultimate customer.

Grand Strategy—We will take this as given. As an SBO you want to maximize your health, wealth and well being as you define them. This is a function of your values.

In the context of this book, SaLT is my product. Choose the acronym that you like and you can find a similar book or product like it. My widget is SaLT tailored to your individual needs. I provide service through perspective; I help you get what you want: You want an executable Grand Strategy.

SaLT's value added:

1. Knowledge
2. Perspective

I define perspective as seeing the SBO for who he/she is, not who he/she *thinks* they are. It is the most value I can give you. According to *Oxford*, perspective is "a mental view of the relative importance of things."

Let's describe in general terms, specifically (yes this is an oxymoron) who you are and some of the problems you face.

The three general types of PWS:

1. You may be more like a retailer or distributor. You are the place for things that are difficult for the big boys to provide. Think, "niche."
2. You may be more like a manufacturer. You make widgets that no one else can make, especially compared to the big boys. Think, "niche."
3. You may be more like a service provider. You could arrange, process, or help find things. You may help the big boys find what they need. Think, "niche."

Your niche may be geographic differentiation, product differentiation or a combination of both.

The three general types of market are:

1. Local to your town or hamlet: perhaps to a neighborhood or small community of retail consumers or commercial customers.
2. Local to your state or region: perhaps to a community of commercial or retail customers. You serve the state or region where you are located.
3. Local to the globe: perhaps to the global retail or commercial customer.

There are three different types of product/company life cycles we will consider. This is defined by your revenue growth.

1. Grow fast—You are in the fast growth stage of the PWS or business.
2. Grow slow—Maturity is drawing closer. Growth remains the watch-word but it is slowing.
3. Stable—Otherwise known as mature: You have stable revenue with predictable cash flows.

There are three stages of the market as a whole for your PWS.

1. Grow Fast—Fast growing industry overall.
2. Grow Slow—Industry overall is still growing, but growth is slowing.
3. Stable—Mature industry with predictable overall demand.

There are three characterizations of market position.

1. Market Leader—You as the dominant player. You don't worry much about your competitors.
2. Oligopolistic—You are one of a several players that constantly compete with and react to each other.
3. Niche—You have a geographic or product differentiation niche. As long as your niche is preserved, rivals don't disturb you. You are the market leader in your niche.

The three challenges most articulated by the SBO in my own experience:

1. I want to retire but I can't. The business is worth x but I can only get 50% of x. This is a transition/culture issue as discussed in Chapter 1. There is a solution, in fact a SaLT Circle for this.
2. My bookkeeper just stole $100,000 (name an amount) from the business. This is a business process or control issue. There is a solution, in fact a SaLT Circle.
3. This is a tough business. We are always busy, but don't seem to make a lot of money. There is a solution for this, in fact a SaLT Circle.

I have defined and delineated our possible positions. Have I covered every possible scenario, product type, market, industry or company? Of course I have not. You can't analyze a blob.

Of note are items I have or will exclude from my analysis.

I will not analyze investment real estate. It is its own animal. While your business may make a buy or lease decision for your premises, you are not in the Investment Real Estate Business. Investment Real Estate defined as apartments, strip malls, office space, warehouse space and manufacturing space held for lease to third parties. You are not a start-up, which is a new business without any history. There are a couple of exceptions, and SaLT will apply to these exceptions as special cases. You could be a potential SBO buying a stable business. Alternatively, you could purchase a reputable franchise and become a SBO.

SaLT in Practice
Step 2

The Plant Tour

I need a "plant tour." Or put another way, I want to visit the SBO's business in its physical space. As the SBO you are the expert in your PWS. I will never know more than you do. I can bring perspective to you. As I need to learn who you are, before I arrive, I'm going to mystery shop your PWS. This will be without your knowledge, as I want first hand exposure to your PWS, your market, your customer and most importantly, your competitor. I want perspective!

When I arrive at your shop, I will know something about you. The knowledge will not be deep, but I will have a perception concerning who you are. When I visit, I assume that you will put your best foot forward. To retain perspective, I will case your business before my visit and after. I want to see who comes and goes; the condition of the physical space; is there trash in the parking lot? What do the employees drive? What do you drive? Are you on site? Who are your vendors?

I need to read the trade journals you subscribe to. Have you been portrayed in the media? How? I want to read about your industry and your competitors. I want to touch and feel your PWS.

Who will be the first person I see when I walk in the door? A receptionist, a clerk, a greeter, a sales person, you? If I must wait to see you, how will I be treated? I will go to great pains to dress as you do. I don't want to be a suit walking into a denim place. Nor do I want to walk in wearing jeans in a suit place. If my wait is long, why is it? Am I made comfortable? Am I offered refreshment as I wait?

How do you greet me? Do you treat me like a peer? If you want to start the tour in receiving, I want to start somewhere else just to throw you off guard. How do you interact with your employees? How do they react to you? Is the front office tidy? How organized is it? How is the shop floor laid out? Is it tidy? Let's look at that incredible new piece of machinery that you just installed. Can we watch a production set-up? How does it work? What does it do for you? Are the employees anxious when running it? Are they proud? I want to meet the shop steward; the plant manager; the sales guy; a line employee: Who does the cleaning? Can I meet the janitor?

Let's look at the front office; Meet the Accounts Receivable (A/R) person; The payable clerk; The inventory person; Show me how a payment is processed; How a check is cut; I'd like to see the checkbook; Meet the accountant; Meet the auditor, The Lawyer.

Can we meet your biggest customer? How about your biggest vendor? Can I chat with them alone? How is your PWS sold? Delivered? Through which channel or channels is it sold?

Let's look at your financial statements? Why are sales up? Down? What drives profit? Do you have a loss leader? How do you calculate gross profit? How does that relate to job cost? Do you bid? Offer a set price? Offer discounts for volume? How do you feel about leverage? Where do you borrow your money? How did you finance that new piece of equipment? Did the manufacturer finance it? Did the bank?

I have described the plant tour this way because I'm trying to learn your business. I'm trying to be the SBO. I'm trying to be you, but with one difference. The difference is that I want to retain my perspective. Not only am I trying to learn your business, but also I am attempting to accomplish one more thing.

Do the things you say agree with what I see? One of the most difficult things for people to do is be self-critical. To be your own Devil's Advocate. It isn't a fault of yours. It is human nature.

How do you gain perspective?

1. Buy it
2. Develop it yourself

In a sense you have bought a small piece of perspective in purchasing this book. Alternatively, you can buy a canned software package to ask the same questions that I have.[110]

You could hire a consultant to help you. You can try to develop it on your own, but it is a difficult task. What is it they say about the insane person? He doesn't know that he's insane. If he knows that he is insane, he probably isn't. Paranoid perhaps, but not insane.

> "The wisest of all, in my opinion, is he who can, if only once a month, call himself a fool."
> —Fyodor Dostoevsky in *Bobok*.[111]

> "It is awfully easy to be hard-boiled about everything in the daytime, but at night it is another thing."
> —Ernest Hemingway in *The Sun Also Rises*.[112]

These quotes by Dostoevsky and Hemingway illustrate two ways, one directly, the other indirectly, that you can strive to develop perspective on your own. Dostoevsky could be interpreted to mean that you should ridicule your assumptions to see if they still hold true. Hemingway makes the point that is hard to remain self-confidant in the middle of the night when self-doubt creeps in. You could examine those doubts and analyze them to determine if they are valid as opposed to simply dismissing them. Either exercise is a way to develop and retain perspective.

SaLT Concept

Develop perspective through self-criticism. Ridicule your assumptions. Try the lens of SaLT for a fresh look at your business.

SaLT in Practice
Step 3

Answer 2 Questions, Get a SaLT Circle

Answer the following questions from Step 1:

1. There are three stages of the market as a whole for your PWS. Which is yours? Choose growth or mature to best describe your situation.
2. There are three characterizations of market position. Which is yours? Choose oligopoly or niche.

Figure Step 3.1—Decision Matrix for Small Business

Market position	Growth Industry	Mature Industry
Oligopoly	SaLT Circle: Find Niche	SaLT Circle: Find Niche
Niche	SaLT Circle: Keep Niche	SaLT Circle: Keep Niche

Decision types are based upon the BCG Model.

We discussed the Boston Consulting Group Model and others in Chapter 11. To refresh, academic models based upon market share, growth rate and competitive position map the strategic decision for businesses. In those models, small business is generally considered a Dog and should be divested. Small business by definition can't be General Electric, Microsoft or Wal-Mart, and your market power is considered weak. Basically as a small business, the models indicate that if you have a niche—defend it. If you don't have a niche—find it. If you can't find a niche—get out. Your basic indication of strategic focus is defined by how you perceive your competitors.

How do you perceive competitors?

Years ago, I had a small business customer who was getting up in years. He had a very opulent office with a big leather chair in front of his desk and a comfortable couch off to the side. When I visited his office, I wanted to sit on the couch. Not only was it more comfortable, but when you sat in the chair you sunk down and had the feeling that Floyd was lording over you. Every time I visited him he would make a big deal for me to sit in the chair. One morning I was a bit cranky so I plopped down on the couch and Floyd started in again. I asked him what was the deal with the chair? He explained that he used to be quite a ladies man so he kept a sawed-off shotgun mounted in the leg well of the desk aimed at the chair. He kept it there in case an angry husband visited him.

I didn't believe him so I asked to see the gun. He fiddled under the desk for a moment and brought out the shotgun that had a short piece of string tied to the trigger. I went around behind to see how it was mounted. He had a cradle with a brace so it could be fired from the well, and it was aimed at the chair. He showed me that it was loaded although the shells were a little green. I claimed he was too old to worry about husbands, so why did he keep the gun? Floyd replied, "I keep it for bankers and difficult competitors." He offered me the couch to sit on but made the point that he had used it in his day to conquer his quests. I was caught between the devil and the deep blue sea on this one. I could have a loaded gun aimed at my chest or sit where he had fornicated. I didn't raise his rate that day or cause any other trouble. In Floyd's case, he knew who his competitors were and had a method to handle them.

The growth-share matrix, is it art or science? Scott Armstrong and Roderick Brodie, in "Effects of Portfolio Planning on Decision Making," evaluate issues in the application of growth-share matrices. They conducted a series of experiments where a group of participants was given the BCG matrix and another group more basic decision rules used in finance such as net present value. The asked the groups to make an identical business decision. They found that the BCG group consistently made a less optimal decision than the group that was given more basic decision models. Criticism of all matrices centered on the following issues:[113]

1. The matrices assume a causal relationship between profit and market share.
2. The matrices only provide a "rule of thumb" as a decision aid.

As the SaLT method is presented, profitability is considered as part of the decision process. As to criticism of a "rule of thumb"[114] approach, I embrace it. Again, in a complex world, one cannot consider every variable. This is exactly the point of satisficing. We are overwhelmed with information and must mentally budget our time.[115] For example in researching the BCG model at the public library for this book, I consulted five texts, three papers and my notes from B-school. The stack of information digested was over twelve inches tall! That information was condensed to present the reader with a few practical paragraphs of decision analysis.

To answer the question, is it art or science? If it is science there is little the small businessperson can add to value to earn his living. If not for his experience, judgment, expertise and gut feeling, what does he offer the market? If it is pure science, let's ask Salesforce.com to sell us a solution subscription to earn money and we can retire to the islands. If it is pure art, then rationality doesn't exist. To answer, it is both. The world is gray. The authors do say that perhaps the matrices lead managers to make less irrational decisions, and matrices were a good starting point in making strategic decisions.[116] I concur.

SaLT Concept

The world is gray. Use black and white to illuminate obstacles.

SᴀLT ɪɴ Pʀᴀᴄᴛɪᴄᴇ
Sᴛᴇᴘ 4

Do you have a Niche?
Feets Neat Company

To start, let's examine some small businesses that have a niche and what this niche is. These are examples of niches in my local area that I patronize, have worked with, have analyzed, have lent money to or pursued as clients. I will not give their names and have changed details as needed to protect their anonymity.

- Nearly any profession such as doctors, lawyers, accountants, optometrists, veterinarians, *et cetera*. They have both a specialized niche due to their training and also a geographic niche.
- Contractor that repairs railways. His niche is both geographic and product as he is not unionized and a minority.
- Wholesale distributor of fabric. The niche is product variety.
- Bottle manufacturer. He also produces machinery to make bottles in small lots. The niche is geographic and product.
- Logistics company serving the small business. The niche is geographic.
- Print shops. The niche is geographic and product.
- Retailer of western wear in the form a super store. The niche is product and geographic.
- Retailer of western wear. The niche is geographic.
- Dry cleaner. Niche is geographic.
- Electronics store. The niche is geographic and product.
- Sports shoe retailer. Niche is geographic and product.
- Job-shop widget makers. Geographic and product niche.
- Widget manufacturers. They have a patent. The niche is product.

♦ Sunglasses distributor to convenience stores. Both product and geographic.
♦ Widget manufacturer. They have a specialized product.
♦ Grocery store. Niche is product and geographic.
♦ Convenience stores. Geographic niche
♦ A Temporary agency. The niche is their Rolodex. Both product and geographic.
♦ Executive placement firm. The niche is their Rolodex. Both product and geographic.

This list is not comprehensive, but merely meant to illustrate niches. They are ones that stand out from my experience for one reason or another.

Oxford defines niche as, "an appropriate combination of conditions for a species to thrive." If we replaced the word species with business, the biological definition would be valid for a small business. In Step 1, we used the word niche several times. In determining market position, we touched upon the notion that having a niche means that you aren't worried about rivals' actions. Let's cast some hypothetical situations to illustrate the point. I will use a retail model for analysis, as it is common to all whether or not you are a retail business. On a personal level you patronize a retail establishment every day. This device will ease analysis.

In a way, cast in economic terms, a niche is a micro-monopoly. If you truly have a great niche, you have very little direct competition. **The word "direct" is key here.**

Imagine you are a retailer of specialty shoes for walking. You carry every walking shoe made. People drive from all over town to buy walking shoes from you. Some even drive from a nearby city to shop at your store. You are the only A to Z walking shoe retailer in the area. You offer personal service to fit the shoes. Your father was a podiatrist, so you know feet. You can distinguish between a bunion, a corn and planter's wart with merely a glance. Clubfoot? No problem. You have the perfect solution. Business is so brisk that you are thinking of selling online on a more limited basis. You know from experience that a foot issue needs your personal attention for proper fitting, but online you could sell a more run of the mill shoe to capitalize on your reputation. Stinky feet? No problem. You have the perfect shoe. Your motto is, "Feet don't stink—people do!" The name of your store: Feets Neat Company.

Let's list some other sellers of walking shoes and imagine how well they compete with Feets?

Wal-Mart—They carry a couple of low-end walking shoes at a discount.
Target—They carry a couple of mid-level walking shoes at a good price.
Sporting goods store—They have 3 high-end shoes at a high price.
Hiking store—They carry 6 high-end, high-price shoes.
Just for Feet—They carry a high-end walking shoe and a low-end walking shoe at a decent price
Department store—They don't carry any walking shoes.
Feets—You carry dozens in all price categories for every conceivable circumstance that one would need walking shoes.

In this hypothetical world, no other retailer provides **direct** competition. If Wal-Mart, *et al.* opened a store next door, you wouldn't care because they offer no direct competition. At least in your town, you have a micro-monopoly on walking shoes. There is no substitute for your store.

Let's expand the example and assume a cobbler opens shop next door. The cobbler has sensed a weakness in your niche. You don't custom-make walking shoes. Suppose a customer had legs of different length with a left and right foot of different sizes. Could Feets accommodate that customer? Feets probably could not accommodate this very rare customer. Would the cobbler next door prove to be a threat to your niche? Probably not, as the universe of customers needing this particular product would be tiny. While the cobbler could make a business from custom-building the proper shoe and charging a lot of money for it, it will not hurt your business. You still have a micro-monopoly.

Let's add another scenario. Fred has noticed that you have a virtual monopoly, and he decides to open a store next to you and share in your fortune. Fred, like you, feels that feet don't stink. He opens Fred's Foot Company right next door. He has the same level of expertise, the same product line and the same passion for feet. Everything is the same. What will happen? We are back to our dry cleaner example in Chapter 8. You now have a direct competitor. You are no longer a micro-monopoly and must consider oligopolistic behavior and game theory. The most likely outcome is that Fred's Foot and Feets will fight tooth-and-nail until you split the market. All things being equal, you will earn half the profit as before. While your name and reputation could give you an advantage in the short-run, in the long-run this advantage will disappear. Can you both exist on half the market? Let's examine different paths:

Outcome 1—Fred's Foot or Feets will exit the market. Do either have the ability to drive out or outwear the other? That will be a function of staying power. If you both have equal resources, you will split the market.

Outcome 2—You and Fred's could collude and split the market at near what you charged before and retain profitability. The temptation to cheat would be high and the collusion would probably break down over time. As was illustrated in Chapter 8, markets tend to gravitate toward oligopolistic forms. In this scenario, you still have half the market with lower profit. If you and Fred's Foot did successively collude, you would eventually attract another player to contend with, as you would still be charging high prices.

Outcome 3—At half the market can you cover fixed costs and still earn a sufficient return? Is there a way to cut costs? Let's assume you split the market. Before Fred's Foot you earned, on a variable cost basis, $0.30 for every dollar sold. Variable costs are $0.70 per dollar or unit. If you sold 1,000 shoes per month at a $1 per shoe, you would earn $300 on a variable basis to cover fixed costs. If fixed costs are $150 per month, your net is $150 per month. When Fred's Foot enters you split volume. You now sell 500 shoes per month at the same margin or price. Your gross profit is $150 per month to cover $150 per month in overhead. Your new net profit is zero. I am simplifying to illustrate the issue. Obviously you could choose any combination of volume-price to reflect the retention of half the market. Can you cut overhead from $150 per month? Does Fred's Feet have the same overhead?

If you can answer the following three questions in the negative, you have three possible SaLT Circles. Keep your perspective as you answer.

1. Do you feel you have a direct competitor in the market?
2. Do you worry as to your rival's actions?
3. Are you a price taker in your market versus a price maker?

If you have no direct competitor, you don't worry about your rival's actions and you are a price maker: You have three possible SaLT Circles:

SaLT Circle 4.1—Protect your niche and pay attention to costs
SaLT Circle 4.2—Adjust scale
SaLT Circle 4.3—Get out of the business

The next question is, are you profitable and/or profitable enough?

If the answer is yes, SaLT Circle 4.1 is yours!

SaLT Circle 4.1 is to protect your niche and pay attention to costs. You have a viable, profitable niche. You should focus on preserving that niche. How do you do this? You must answer that question. I do not know your business like you do. If I did offer a solution without the specifics of your business, it would not apply to all products or industries. This book stops at the water's edge of specifics. In general, I can say that you should harbor your resources. In addition, focus on costs and internal controls and remain aware, perceptive and flexible to address challenges as they arrive. The most important of those listed is to harbor your resources. As in the illustration of tactics in Chapter 12, in a street fight, all things being equal, the stronger opponent will win. In the same way, your business should build its strength, its resources and its capital.

Inherent to SaLT 4.1, you could create your niche in another locale. Open another store in another part of town, or the next city, or the next state, or sell on the Internet. You could also franchise your model to others and earn a fee and royalties. These have an entirely different set of SaLT Circles.

If you answer the question about profitability in the negative, you should consider adjusting your scale. This will be discussed in Step 5. If you can't adjust scale to create your viable, profitable niche, you should consider exiting the business. This is not presented as a straw man. A straw man is an imaginary option to illustrate a position. This is a real option painful as it is to contemplate. If you have a niche, but can't make it profitable or profitable enough to fit your needs, you may be wasting your time and needlessly risking your capital.

Ram Charan, in "Sharpening Your Business Acumen," and Donald L. Laurie, *et al.*, in "Creating New Growth Platforms," discuss ways to refocus your business. These articles address the titans of the business world, but I have adapted their conclusions for the small business.

Ram Charan, in "Sharpening Your Business Acumen," asks six questions[117] that may help sharpen your focus. As I have adapted, they become five and include:

1. What is happening in my niche today?

How is the niche changing? What trends are emerging as it relates to the product, delivery, and service? Who is hot in the niche?

2. What does it mean to my customer?

How does my customer interact with the niche as it changes? What does the customer find of value?

3. What does it mean to my business?

How does my business fit in this changing niche? Should I change the product, distribution, service, or cost structure of production to better fit the niche?

4. How can I connect trends in the niche to the customer?

Where are the strengths and weakness of the niche? Where is my profit derived? How does my mix of product, delivery, service and cost structure fit with what the customer wants?

5. What are the operational strategies to connect the niche, to the customer, to my business?

What logistics and tactics will allow me to connect with the customer? What is the first step? What are the second, third or fourth steps?

Donald L. Laurie, *et al.*, in "Creating New Growth Platforms," envision a growth platform as a convergence of zones[118] to identify where one should focus. In my adaptation for the small business, I see the zones as follows:

Figure Step 4.1—Alignment

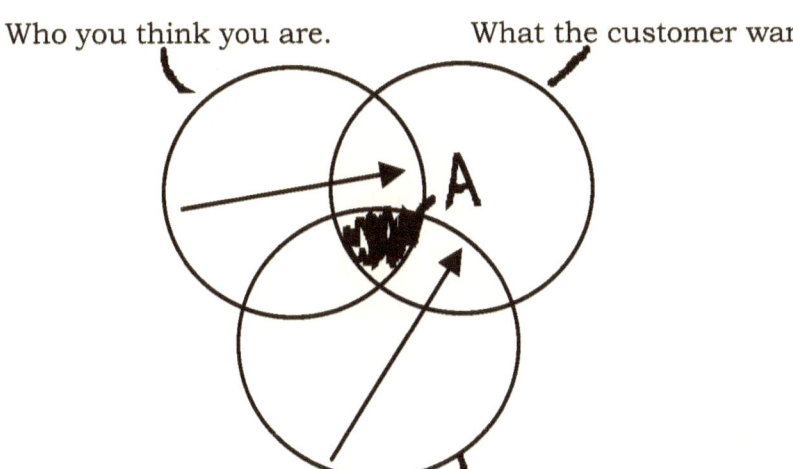

Who you think you are.   What the customer wants.

Who you actually are.

The authors point to the shaded area labeled A. This is where your focus should be in looking for new growth in your market. It is where the circles converge. I see the solution as a realignment of your business with your niche. I contend that over time, you expect a divergence of what the customer wants, who you think you are, and who you actually are. This is human nature and impossible to escape. The point is you should try to realign the three so that the circles lie on top of one another again. The arrows point into the direction you want to move. It is up to your business to align with the customer. It is not the customer's responsibility. In the end an ideal outcome would be one circle encompassing all three ideas.

Regina E. Herzlinger, in "Why Innovation in Healthcare Is So Hard," discusses six reasons for the difficulty of realignment. They include players, funding, policy, technology, customers and accountability. She points out that the healthcare industry has been particularly resistant to product and delivery innovation.[119] I've adapted the reasoning for application to Figure Step 4.1. The following roadblocks exist for the small business as they realign:

1. Culture, employee, SBO—In corporate culture, the employees or the SBO himself may be resistant to change. This may be a function of ignorance, arrogance or simply stagnation. A good example is my local high-end butcher. He has an excellent product at premium prices but he will not under any circumstance accept a credit card for payment. He will only accept cash or a personal check. I rarely carry sufficient cash for a $40 to $50 purchase and never carry a checkbook. This is precisely the reason I carry credit cards. I've asked the butcher several times why he won't take plastic, and his response is that he just doesn't like it. It has become a running joke between us. I can think of several reasons why he may not want to accept credit cards and that is his choice. I do know that I don't patronize him as often as I want to because of the difficulty in payment. I would contend he could double his volume at current price with his current facilities by simply adding the convenience of accepting credit cards.

2. Regulation and economies of scale—Regulation or scale issues may prevent the business from realigning its platform. In Oklahoma, peculiarities of our liquor laws prevent grocers from selling wine. This prevents our state from having boutique groceries. Boutique grocers in other states offer a high-end niche product and often rely on wine sales to support the lower margin grocery business.

3. Technology—Often, product realignment may require a technology solution or implementation of technology that already is standard. A company that isn't technologically savvy is at a disadvantage. The widget maker in a job shop or manufacture to spec business immediately comes to mind. On many occasions, I've witnessed SBOs that cost jobs and price based upon their gut feel. A job costing system could easily alleviate the problem of underestimating costs and under pricing a product or product line. I've seen manufacturers produce themselves out of business by unintentionally accepting a large contract at or below cost. Technology is not the end all solution but it pays to be conversant with what is available.

4. Customer sophistication—Customers are increasingly more sophisticated. As a small business, you probably aren't the low-price leader but rely on service. Customers increasingly see through lip service as it relates to customer service and will take their business elsewhere. *Customer service will in all likelihood make or break your platform as it is the value you add.* My favorite peeve is to call a customer service phone line only to play the "press this number" game. If I expect face to face service from the small business I patronize and don't get it, I may as

well go to a larger provider and pay less. The local business logistics firm I patronize would not long retain my business if they didn't cater to my personal needs. I can go elsewhere and be treated as one of the herd for 25% less.

SaLT Concept

It is important to consider these four roadblocks and their possible interplay with your business as you realign your platform.

SaLT in Practice
Step 5

Adjusting Scale

We need to define fixed and variable costs for this step. Fixed costs are items like rent, interest, mortgage payments, insurance, administration, *et cetera*. They do not vary with volume in the short-run. Variable costs are not fixed and they vary with volume. This is generally thought of as cost of sales. Gross profit is sales less cost of sales. Gross profit divided by sales is gross profit margin.

Using Feets Neat as our example, the graphic depiction of fixed versus variable is as follows.

Graph—SaLT Step 5.1—Fixed v. Variable

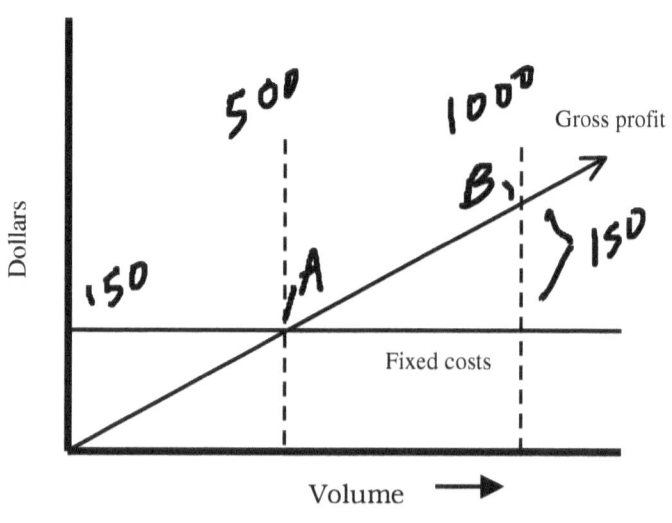

Feets' fixed costs are $150, gross margin is 30% and sales are $1 per unit. At 500 shoes sold, gross profit is $150, fixed costs are $150 and net profit is zero. At 1,000 shoes sold, Gross profit is $300, fixed costs are $150 and net profit is $150. Point A denotes zero net profit. Point B denotes $150 net profit. To increase profit, you either charge more (shift gross profit up) or lower fixed costs (shift down). When you shift the curves, I call this "adjusting scale." If your SaLT Circle is 4.2, a niche but not profitable, you either need to raise prices charged or lower costs.

SaLT Circle 4.2 dictates a change in scale. Can you increase volume? Can you effectively advertise or market to increase volume? This could mean sending salesmen to sales school, implement a sales strategy, manage the sales process, attend more trade shows, advertise in the media, hold sales promotions, *et cetera*. Effective means the benefit outweighs the cost of the sales strategy. Can you successfully raise price? Unless you have a control or system issue, you are probably charging what the market can bear. Control or system issues are usually the domain of widget makers. Their cost-accounting systems are somehow flawed and they fail in properly job-costing and pricing accordingly. A solution here would be to hire a job-cost guru to sort out the issues or implement a system. Often widget makers do not have a system other than the SBO's best guess. Simple implementation of a job cost system can solve this issue.

If you buy inventory as finished goods, can you negotiate better price or terms with the supplier say related to volume? This would be a reasonable way to increase margin. Could you shed a product line if it is unprofitable? This would be a way to raise margin. In addition, you could reduce carrying costs and use the free cash to pay debt and the related interest. This would lower fixed costs.

Finally, could you reduce overhead or fixed costs? You could pay down debt, negotiate better lease terms with the landlord, reduce wages by cutting unneeded staff, look at insurance costs or generally turn off the lights at night to reduce overhead.

What if you can't seem to do what SaLT Circle 4.2 prescribes? You can't seem to adjust scale. There is another way left open by the nature of fixed costs. In Chapter 5 we said economics tried to smooth the lumps. Fixed costs can be lumpy and they can be quasi-fixed.

Graph—SaLT Step 5.2—Lumpy Fixed Costs

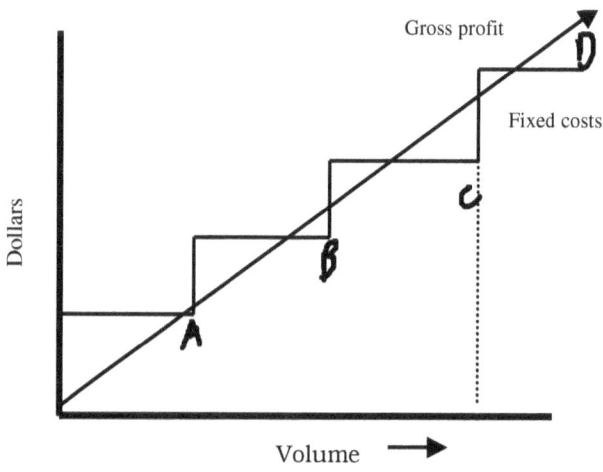

The stair step curve indicates lumpy fixed costs. All things being equal, lumpiness indicates that a business may have a natural size. At point A, volume allows for no profitability. Point B allows a small window. Points C and D offer a larger range of profitability. Point C appears to be the optimal maximum natural size. The next graph most accurately represents how costs behave in the in the real world. Because both fixed and variable cost can be lumpy and quasi-fixed or quasi-variable, the lines are no longer linear.

Graph—SaLT Step 5.3—Real World

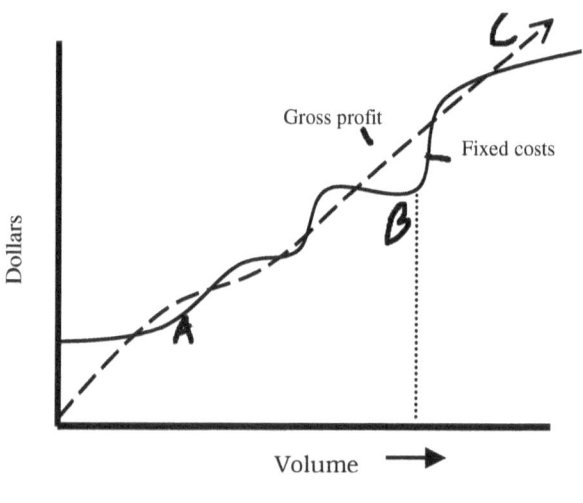

Again, gross profit is represented by the line with the arrow and is dashed. It implies different profitability margins at different points on the curve. The solid line represents fixed costs. Opportunities for profitability occur at Points A, B and C. In Graph 5.3, Point B would seem to be the optimal, maximum, natural size.

In order to adjust your scale, given Graph 5.3, you need to either contract or grow to this optimal size. Sometimes more volume is detrimental to the bottom line. In addition, assuming you moved to Point B and had a geographic niche, you could either add additional locations or franchise your business. How to adjust the business to the optimal size is very difficult to articulate in general terms. The particular way would be so industry and product specific that a general rule could not be adapted. Again, as SBO, you are the expert. Reverting back to our dry-cleaner example, an intersection may offer one size for profitability. But you could expand by opening in a different part of town on the same scale and have multiple stores.

Kaj Grichnik, *et al.*, in "Manufacturing Myopia," discusses strategies large companies use to realign costs and the outcomes of those strategies. The authors cite four strategies.[120]

Option 1—Locally controlled cuts, which I term the "grass roots" strategy. Consult with shop floor, and consensus is achieved. Costs are usually cut in the short run, with no strategic shift in business.

Option 2—Centrally controlled cuts, which I term "fire every 10th worker." Goal can be achieved but leads to unfairness and passive aggressive behavior by employees. No strategic shift is achieved.

Option 3—Selective cuts dictated by certain business metrics. Key performance indicators dictate cuts. The desired outcome can be achieved but the result is short-term with no strategic shift.

Option 4—I call "strategic integration." Priority driven cuts based upon overall strategy. It necessitates a review of strategic objectives and competitive position, and leads to long-term strategic changes and cost cutting. In theory, it should increase quality, speed and service advantages.

Option 4 appears to be the most effective option in the long-run especially given the discussion of Figure Step 4.1. It also requires more discipline and thought, but could place your business in the advantage as it adapts to challenges.

The bottom line is this, if you feel you have a niche and aren't satisfied with the profitability, adjust your scale. If this is not possible, you are either the proverbial buggy-whip maker or have not judged your position accurately. In fact, the buggy-whip maker has not disappeared into history. A company based in New Zealand makes buggy whips for harness racing. The Zilco 'Westfield' Whip with closed flapper can be purchased for $59.95 plus shipping.[121] If you can't become Zilco,[122] then Dante is appropriate as you enter the gates of hell:

> Through Me Pass into the Painful City,
> Through Me Pass into Eternal Grief,
> Through Me Pass among the Lost People.
> Justice Moved My Master-Builder:
> Heavenly Power First Fashioned Me
> With Highest Wisdom and with Primal Love.
> Before Me Nothing Was Created That
> Was Not Eternal, and I Last Eternally.
> All Hope Abandon, You Who Enter Here.—Dante. *Inferno*, Canto III.
> Inscribed on the gates of hell.[123]

Westfield, Massachusetts was known in 1865 as the buggy-whip capital of the world. Called "Whip City," it had 95% of the domestic whip market. In 1893, at it peak, 80% of the town was employed by the industry. The advent of the automobile decimated demand for carriage whips. By World War Two, only two companies held out.[124] Because braiding was a process used in whip manufacture, local business began braiding fishing line in the 1930's. U.S. Whip, a leader in whips, renamed itself U.S. Line.[125] A Google search revealed that U.S. Line Company based in Westfield is a distributing company that distributes and manufactures fishing line and employs less than 49 employees. The company was founded in 1924.

SaLT in Practice Step 6

You Lost Your Niche

I hear hurricanes a-blowing
I know the end is coming soon
I fear rivers over flowing
I hear the voice of rage and ruin

—From "Bad Moon Rising."
lyrics by John Fogerty[126]

What does SaLT prescribe if you have lost your niche or you now have a direct competitor? In the Feets Neat example we added a direct competitor to the mix: Fred's Foot. What is an appropriate SaLT in this instance? The most likely outcome, assuming the market or your actions allow you both to coexist, is a Nash Equilibrium. A Nash Equilibrium as discussed in Chapter 8, is a collective strategy in a game involving two or more players, where no player has anything to gain by changing only his or her own strategy. Your game playing skill will be instrumental in reaching equilibrium. After the entrance of Fred's, Feets will earn less profit on less volume than before Fred's entered. The strategic decision tree prescribes that you find your niche. In this case your SaLT is the following:

SaLT 6.1—Lost niche, find new niche, settle in equilibrium. As assumed in this scenario, enough market exists for Feets and Fred's to coexist. You would not be able to drive Fred's from your market. In general, the specific steps needed are:

1. Distinguish your product from Fred's. Engage in non-price competition. Enhance revenue with effective marketing.
2. Cut costs using the activities discussed in Step 6. Rationalize pricing. Nurture and protect product lines that are more profitable. Seek to minimize unprofitable lines. Be conscious of your loss leader.
3. Be very attentive to price and careful of price-cutting. As cautioned in Chapter 8, avoid arbitrary action.
4. Signal Fred's that you are willing to settle in equilibrium. I don't mean collude, as it is illegal, but foster a cooperative spirit knowing that you will coexist.
5. Play the game, utilizing your game playing skills.
6. Most importantly, prepare for the next entrant. Since you and Fred's will settle in equilibrium that implies that enough economic surplus exists for your both. Economics indicates that the market will recognize this surplus and another direct competitor will enter the stage. Harbor your resources.

If you lose your niche due to the entrance of direct competition and you can't settle in equilibrium, your SaLT circle looks very similar to SaLT Circle 4.2. Follow the steps to adjust scale in Step 5. If this is not successful, consider exiting stage left.

Economics classifies fixed costs or "money out the door" as irrelevant to future decision making. Sunk costs should be ignored in evaluating what to do tomorrow. In the small businessperson's case, if the decision is to abandon a business, the investment in time, money and prestige should be ignored in the decision process. This is difficult to do. In their article, "The Sunk Cost and Concorde Effects: Are Humans Less Rational Than Lower Animals?" Hal R. Arkes and Peter Ayton make the following points:

> The sunk cost effect is a maladaptive economic behavior that is manifested in a greater tendency to continue an endeavor once an investment in money, effort or time has been made. The Concorde fallacy is another name for the sunk cost effect, except that the former has been applied strictly to lower animals, whereas the latter has been applied solely to humans. The authors contend that there are no unambiguous instances of the Concorde fallacy in lower animals and also evidence exist that young children, when placed in an economic situation akin to a sunk cost one, exhibit more normatively correct behavior than do adults.[127]

The authors point out that the name Concorde fallacy was related to the development of the Concorde supersonic passenger jet. Early on it was determined that it wasn't economically viable but the sponsoring countries felt they have too much prestige invested in the project to walk away from it.[128] They also share two reasons why people may continue to regard sunk costs in decision making. The first is our value set frowns upon wastefulness.[129] The second is that humans associate past investment with future benefit. This decisional shortcut or bias could outweigh the cost of using a more [conceptually] cumbersome but correct rule to ignore sunk cost.[130]

SaLT in Practice
Step 7

SaLT Decision Tree

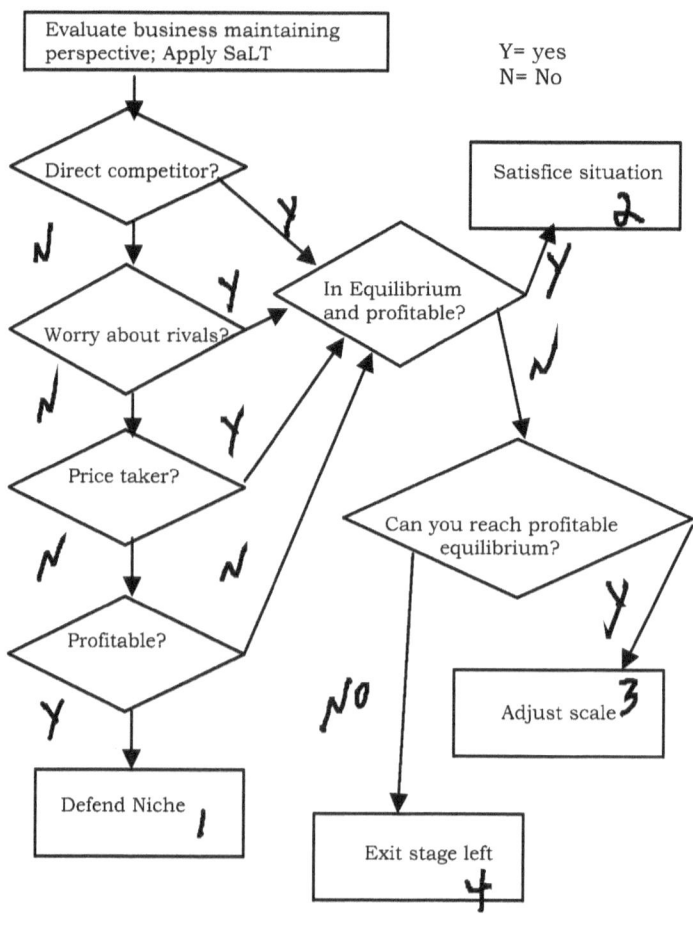

Your possible choices with SaLT are:

1. Defend Niche and Maximize
2. Satisfice
3. Adjust Scale
4. Exit Stage Left

You should continually start at the top of the tree as time passes. If you are like Tulsa Sound in our example in Chapter 15, you should not have entered the market in the first instance. Given that you did, you should plan an exit with the least negative consequence.

SaLT in Practice
Special Issues

In Step 1, I alluded to three common questions and a special case for evaluating start-ups and franchisee opportunities. Those will be covered in this section.

> Trouble ahead, trouble behind,
> And you know that notion just crossed my mind.
> Trouble with you is the trouble with me,
> Got two good eyes but we still don't see.
> Come round the bend, you know its the end,
> The fireman screams and the engine just gleams.
> —From "Casey Jones." lyrics by Robert Hunter.[131]

The three challenges most articulated by the SBO in my own experience:

Challenge 1. I want to retire but I can't. The business is worth x but I can only get 50% of x.

In many instances, the SBO and the business are so intertwined that it is difficult separating the two. In Chapter 1, I discussed the founder's role and the growth of corporate culture. If the SBO and the business are intertwined, it is difficult to sell the business as a going concern as the business will wither without the SBO. A SaLT Circle comes to mind for this problem.

SaLT Circle to maximize salability—One alternative is to instill in the company a corporate culture reflective of your own. This means articulating you values and vision to those in the business and sharing customer relationships in the form of delegating the sales function to others. This is more easily done in retail where a standardized product is sold and more difficult for the widget maker. Many times the widget maker has specialized knowledge about the product and/or special relationships with the customer that are unique to the SBO. In this way, as you exit, the business can continue as a going concern without you. You could also court a purchaser and coach the potential SBO that would purchase the business as to its intricacies. This strategy does have risks. As you disengage, you become less important to the future of the company. You also run the risk of a key employee or suitor with your specialized information starting his own business. Institutional controls are of greater concern as you disengage. However, if you want to disengage from the business and maximize its selling price, this would accomplish the goal.

On the retail end of the spectrum, franchising your model would be a way to maximize your pay-out. As you institutionalize the model, its systems and controls the business becomes more salable. In addition, you could set up the franchise in an entity you own selling the franchise of the original and subsequent outlets reaping the fee and ongoing royalties.

Challenge 2. My bookkeeper just stole $100,000 from the business.

This is not uncommon in small businesses with an overextended SBO. I have on more than one occasion lent an owner out of this situation which was life-threatening to the business. It is the quintessential dilemma of having Marge, the office manager for 20 years, cooking the books on you. The SaLT Circle for this is to implement controls into the business. The simplest solution is to have your books audited by an independent accounting firm and heed its suggestions for controls. If the problem is more complex than this, you may need to upgrade accounting firms to one experienced enough to address the issues.

While the cost of an audit seems large, if the business is large enough to afford it, it will pay off in the long run. You can afford 10 years of accounting fees to offset a $100,000 loss to a book cooker. In addition, after the fraud is found you will end up having audits forced upon you probably at greater cost than you could have originally engaged the auditor. It will also help you in addressing Challenge 1 above. Remember, Marge isn't necessarily a "bad" person, but in accounting they say, "need plus opportunity creates fraud."

Challenge 3. I have too little production or conversely, not enough business.

This is the scale issue that I flowcharted and explained for you. It is exceedingly common.

Start-ups take three forms: a complete start from scratch, a SBO-Suitor arrangement of purchasing the business from the current owner or a franchise opportunity. The principles are the same, but I will pay more attention to franchise opportunities as they offer more data and numbers to crunch. There is also a "market" to assess their value.

> She's been looking like a queen in a sailor's dream
> And she don't always say what she really means
> Sometimes I think it's a shame
> When I get feeling better when I'm feeling no pain.
> —From "Sundown." lyrics by Gordon Lightfoot[132]

The lyrics to "Sundown" articulate a problem with perspective when reviewing start-up opportunities. Like the queen in the sailor's dream, once ashore for a few days the queen may not look as appealing to the sober sailor as on that first night ashore. It takes a bit of half-full thinking when considering a start-up, and rightly so. You still have to approach it from a sober point of view.

In my own case, in the last 12 months I evaluated a franchise opportunity for my own account. I went through the same process that I will articulate and in the end decided not to pursue the opportunity. The numbers worked, but in the end what the franchiser told me and an item on their financial statement did not seem to agree, so I decided to pass. It was an agonizing decision and the franchiser didn't make it any easier by calling frequently and applying subtle pressure. I feel confident that I made the right decision, which is a positive to draw from the experience. When I became interested in the opportunity, I mystery shopped an existing outlet before I ever contacted the franchiser. I was able, through several visits, to meet the owner of the outlet and gain insight into his relationship with the franchiser. What I found through mystery shopping was positive.

I spent several thousand dollars investigating the opportunity. I visited the home office and sat in on their training, reviewed controls and practice, spent "a day in the life" at an outlet. I had a contract reviewed by my attorney ready to sign and had the required capital in place. Before I signed, I had a gut-check with the opportunity using my own values and we decided not to pursue. It was a decent opportunity, but ultimately it was in conflict with our values. Had I not been on the bubble about the numbers, our decision may have been different. I use "we" and "our" since it was a family decision. Family is an important concept in my value set.

The following financial analysis will evaluate a dry cleaning opportunity, as I've used a dry cleaner for illustration previously. I did not obtain the financial information from any proprietary source, nor will I tell you the name of the franchiser. I picked this example at random because the public information available included minimum capital requirements. If you are a dry cleaner, you may scoff and decide my numbers are off, but that is not the point. The process is the point.

In your evaluation, first you have to be comfortable with the opportunity and the capital required for it. You also must have access to capital one way or another.

The cost of this hypothetical franchise has a minimum capital and fee requirement of $200,000. It also requires that you have $30,000 on hand to cover the working capital for the start-up phase and $10,000 in order to build out the space. If you can build out for less, you keep the money and can use it for working capital. For your $200,000 you get the franchise, the equipment and installation, training, accounting systems and a marketing package in addition to a protected sales territory. That is, territory protected from another franchisee under the same flag. You must secure the lease on the premises, arrange for and pay any licensing costs, paint and decorate according to agreement and be prepared to open for business within a committed time frame. You also owe the franchiser a quarterly royalty based upon sales.

Assume that I found the following industry information for dry cleaners.

Average annual revenue	$170,000
Gross profit margin	56%
Average annual rent	$12,000
Average annual salaries	$35,000

About the averages: First, I intuitively know that dry cleaners are multiplant. In other words, a particular flag will have several locations around town. A mom and pop store is not the norm. From this we can assume ownership is compensated from the bottom line. The industry data for salaries includes a manager and part-time employee. We can also assume, although industry data does not detail, royalties are reflected in the gross margin number. We would think multiple outlets would have a royalty reflected in the data.

Let's torture the data a bit:

Assuming we would be average, cash flow for the business is gross profit less salary and rent. On an annual basis this number is $95,200 less $12,000 and less $35,000 or a free cash flow of $48,000. Advertising and payroll taxes could reduce this by an additional $10,000 or a grand total of average cash flow of $38,000 annually. What would you be willing to pay for the cash flow? Let's assume a required return by the "market" of 12%. The present value of $38,000 per year in perpetuity at 12% is $317,000.

You could adjust the industry average for several items according to your market. Is it bigger or smaller than average? How much competition exists? Would you open in a new neighborhood or an established one? You would need to use your judgment in this case. In this case, we will rest at average.

How does your estimate of average or likely compare to the franchiser's estimate he has provided to you? If I told you it was 50% of their best case and 75% of their expected case, how would you feel? If your likely case is 25% from their likely case, that isn't too bad. So let's evaluate. If everything goes to plan, the franchiser requires an investment of $240,000 and you value the cash flow at $317,000. Your expected cash flow exceeds your expected costs. This is a positive.

Assume all doesn't go as planned. Assume that you will need a full year of payroll and rent to get it off the ground and running. We calculated these items at $57,000 annually. If you needed a year's fixed costs plus your $210,000 investment that would be an investment of $267,000. Let's assume a higher return adjusted for risk at 14% instead of 12%. Your new amount you would pay for the cash flow is $271,000. So considering a "downside" alternative, the value you pay of $267,000 is about the same as the estimated value you would receive at $271,000. Based upon the numbers, you are even on the decision.

Assuming it is a one-plant operation, your average net after tax will be about 4% of sales or $6,800. We will also assume you work as manager so pay yourself $25,000 for a total salary of $31,800. This of course is before any debt is repaid or capital returned to you. If you have the capital to invest, could you do so and earn the same amount in the stock market with perhaps lower risk? The industry average of debt carried is about $10,000. Do you have the additional $257,000 in capital needed in the downside case? Can you borrow it personally? Experience leads me to believe that after business risk, the main reason new businesses fail is that they are undercapitalized. Of course, you do have the possibility of the upside. If you make the franchiser's best case, your net would be $13,600 plus the $25,000 salary or $38,600 total based upon the industry. The franchiser claims net to you would be $60,000 total with you acting as manager.

SaLT Concept

Now it comes down to how you feel about it. I leave that decision to you.

SaLT in Practice
Continuing Success

Gonna buy me a ticket now, as far as I can,
ain't never comin' back.
Take me Southbound, all the way to Georgia now, till the
train run out of track
> —From "Can't You See." lyrics by Toy Caldwell.[133]

Your business has found its niche and is adequately profitable. Given the caution of looking out for the next competitor, trend, style, preference or technology to infringe on your niche, where do you go from here?

Put in terms of the fishing analogy, do you?

Keep your Bass Tracker
Buy a bigger Bass boat
Buy a Johnboat

Do you stay the size that you are, expand your market for the present model or enter a new market with your cash cow?

If you stay the size you are you may be at a stage in life where you are tired of the fight or want to pursue personal or family interests. As economics will tell us, it is likely that over time your niche will become threatened, and you will have to fight again or exit. Can you harvest enough value from the current model to meet your life goals?

If you expand your model to a larger market or add geographic locations, you are using the cash cow to expand the present model. This has an advantage in that you are an expert in the industry and product that you offer. Be sure the controls are in place so the cow isn't slaughtered while you're in the next pasture. The risk here is similar to the risk of staying in place. The landscape of competition, trend, style, preference or technology may change and threaten your model. Again, the best practice is to have the business in control and be alert and able to react to challenges.

As an alternative, you could use the cow to expand into different businesses and diversify. Diversification will go a long way toward reducing you exposure to current changes in the landscape. However, your expansion is into businesses in which you have a lesser amount of experience. Again, preservation of the cash cow through controls is critical here, but an advantage is that you are a seasoned businessperson.

Your values come intensely in to play in these scenarios. I have worked with two clients that have chosen different paths and remain extremely successful. They are very different personalities and have traveled in completely different directions but have approximately the same amount of wealth.

The first took his model nationwide and has a high profile in his industry. Everything has been invested in the current model and he has done quite well. He lives a grand lifestyle and is accorded deference when he travels. He is a fabulous person who has not been without challenge, but he is engaged, wealthy and happy.

The second client is the exact opposite. He lives modestly and below the radar screen. He has taken his original business and started many others. All three current businesses are in different places on the curve and are successful. This gentleman doesn't have a high profile and you wouldn't guess he has amassed the wealth that he has. Over time he's had a venture or two that didn't perform as he would have liked, but none were "bet the farm" moves. He is also a spectacular person who is engaged, wealthy and happy.

There is no right or wrong answer. It depends upon who you want to be.

SaLT in Practice
Change

"… like the crazy Aunt in the attic."—Drew Altman, Ph.D. on Lyndon Johnson's appreciation of the view that the South was like a "crazy Aunt" when its embrace of racial segregation was considered.[134]

Change is like the crazy Aunt in the attic. If you have a crazy Aunt, and she has one eye in the middle of her forehead, you don't bring her out when company calls. The human animal loathes change. It is wired into our system. Just like we have a Status Quo Bias, we are risk averse. The notion of change frightens us. If change, in fact, only led to positive outcomes, we would not fear it. Change is the embodiment of risk. Risk is an uncertain outcome that I have previously defined. The tools to deal with risk have been articulated by the SaLT method, but let's dig a bit deeper into change.

Motivational snippets, especially those that relate to change, populate our offices and cubes in the form of framed presentations or photocopies tacked on the wall. In my first job, at then a Big 8 accounting firm that no longer exists (think Enron), a colleague had a quote that he loved and had versions of it plastered about his cube. It read:

> Every morning the Lion wakes up and knows it will have to start running and out run the slowest Zebra. If it doesn't: it won't eat. If that happens too many days in a row, the Lion will not survive. The Zebra wakes up every morning and looks around knowing it must get ready to run. The Zebra knows it better out run the fastest Lion or it will not survive. You see it doesn't matter if you are running after something or running from something just make sure you are running.

I always laughed at his embrace of this snippet and tagged him, behind his back, as the "Running Man." It isn't fair to make sport of the Running

Man as we all have our favorite snippets that help us manage life. As Bill W. says, "whatever works." Successories is a very popular purveyor of these snippets. Mac Anderson founded it in 1985 with a group of colleagues to market framed quotations, books and gifts.[135] The snippets are always presented with a breathtakingly appropriate photograph. The company went public in 1990 and reverted to private ownership in 2003. Successories offers snippets related to change that include:[136]

> Learn to embrace change, and you'll begin to recognize that life is in constant motion, and every change happens for a reason. When you see boundaries as opportunities, the world becomes a limitless place, and your life becomes a journey of change that always finds its way.

> If you're not riding the wave of change ... you'll find yourself beneath it.

> Sometimes in the waves of change we find our true direction.

> Change is life giving. It helps us grow into someone greater than we already are.

I will take it as a given that attitude and motivation are vital in developing the courage and perspective to manage change. Let's apply SaLT and find practical steps to manage change in the real world.

Change is inevitable. Nothing stays the same throughout our lives or the life of our business. Significant others, kids, spouses and jobs come and go and evolve over the course of our life. In business, management, demand, supply and fortune change and evolve. It can't be avoided. Change will increase your fortune, leave it the same or lower it. Given that we cannot avoid change, how do we recognize it and manage it in our favor. SaLT prescribes a method to deal with risk and perspective.

To illustrate managing change, a surfing analogy immediately comes to mind; but I don't surf. However, as a kid my family spent a week at the beach every summer, and I was an endless wave rider on my trusty air mattress! This was in the 1970's before boogie boards and similar items were popular or available. My inner consultant feels that "catching a wave" is similar for the kid on an air mattress and the professional surfer. The scale is different, but the principles are the same. When "catching the wave," you take your device offshore where the waves begin their break. You orient toward the shore so you don't lose sight of mom and dad as the current pushes you. Keeping one eye on the shore and one eye on the swells, you adjust your "rhythm" to the cadence of the water. At just the right moment, the wave, you and the device are one. You pull forward and ride the wave to shore. You have executed a successful ride! The steps for successfully managing risk have been articulated in previous chapters, but to recapitulate:

1. Keep your options open
2. Be alert and awake
3. Focus on where you are and where you are going
4. Pray to the god of timing and seize the moment
5. Motivation and attitude are critical in maintaining perspective

Remember. It's just noodles!

Appendices

Introduction

I introduce a case for your decision. I will first give you the background and the decision facing the board of CaseCo in 2003. First, CaseCo will be presented without identifying information if you want to play the game. It is a retail example timely for its current transition. The board decision will be a strategic one and a CEO for CaseCo must be chosen to tactically implement the decision. For simplicity, we will not analyze profitability but will stick to the arena of Grand strategy. It is assumed that if you effectively choose the correct strategy and CEO to implement it, CaseCo will succeed. This is not an unrealistic board decision, but is similar in scope to the decision a corporate board would routinely make. The ultimate outcome of the case is not yet decided as the choice factually made in 2003 was augmented by a successive choice by the board in 2006.

Appendix

CaseCo

CaseCo was founded at the turn of the 20th century and created its niche in the 1920's. Its fame is based upon a reputation of selling luxury goods. Arguably, the apogee of its reputation was cemented in the late 1950's and the avenue was a popular backdrop for films of the time. That era and the backdrop remain my personal preference for the life I wish I could live. However, I was born too late. I'm the quintessential man without a time. Born thirty years tardy for Midtown Manhattan, I'm a year late to be a Boomer and too old for Generation X.

In the mid-1970's, CaseCo was bought by an international conglomerate, and changed hands again in 1990. In 1998, current ownership, a regional retailer, bought the national chain. By the year 2000, the long-time retiring CEO had positioned the store to capitalize on its reputation and had built an impressive in-store label. The new CEO from the regional retailer took the reins and felt that CaseCo needed to expand in smaller markets and lose its "snooty" image. In the interim, prevailing wisdom was the chain had lost it way and was fighting the "ravages of age." Since the 1970's, two successful competitors emerged as direct competition to CaseCo. It is 2003, and the board must decide on a Grand Vision for CaseCo and pick an appropriate person to implement the strategy. Three choices exist:

1. Continue the same path but with a different leader.
2. Reposition to the trendy high-end that was once your fame.
3. Solidify the mature high-end that was your model in the 1970's and 1980's.

What is your Grand Strategic Decision? 1, 2 or 3?
Answer _____

Appendix

Facts
Saks Fifth Avenue

Saks Fifth Avenue was the creation of Horace Saks and Bernard Gimbel. Their vision was to open a unique specialty store that would become the byword for taste and elegance. That main store opened on 5th Avenue in 1924. Adam Gimbel created the Saks Empire and reigned from 1924 to 1969. His intuitive perception was admired as he traveled the world in search of goods that would set Saks apart from the competition. In 1973, Saks was acquired by B.A.T. Industries and Philip B. Miller led the firm until the year 2000. Created in 1985, its "Real Clothes" private label was a major strategic priority that appealed to the loyal 35 to 55 year-old Saks customer. In 1998, Saks merged with Proffitt's, a regional retailer founded in 1919 in Alcoa, Tennessee. The resulting merger in 1998 spun out Proffitt's and Saks as Saks, Incorporated owned by R. Brad Martin. Martin felt Saks needed to venture into smaller markets and lose its "snooty" image.

In 2003, Saks chose Fred Wilson formerly of Donna Karan International to take the helm from Martin. In the 2003 *Times* article, Wilson faced the challenge of reinvigorating the chain. Its stores had been allowed to deteriorate and Wilson was perceived as "a fine merchant." Customer service needed improvement and the merchandise line needed to center around a vision versus a sense of product discontinuity from store to store.

In the 2006 *Times* article, Wilson is criticized for his performance. He eliminated Real Clothes, and courted the younger customer who wanted trendy, skin-bearing fashion. Mr. Wilson compared his vision of Saks to that of BMW telling analysts that Saks must distinguish itself from the Cadillac shopper and appeal to 30-something consumers. Wilson's management style rested upon personality and not strategy or tactics an industry insider noted.

The CEO chosen in 2006, Stephen I. Sadove, has a background in consumer goods as former head of Clairol, a division of Procter and Gamble. The insider mused that Saks needed to return to its mainstream which Sadove was positioned to do. Sadove will reestablish a Private Collections line to cater again to the 35 to 55 year-old with an emphasis on classic style versus trendy and refocus on providing luxury in its sprawling business.

Performance—Saks, Neiman Marcus and Nordstrom

Feb-Mar-Apr same store growth %	Saks	Neiman Marcus	Nordstrom
2006	<2>	7	5
2005	2	8	6
2004	10	13	13
2003	<3>	2	<1>
2002	1	<2>	<1>
Average	2%	6%	4%

Saks has consistently under performed in same store growth versus Neiman Marcus and Nordstrom.

What did the board choose in 2003?

It is not clear precisely what the decision was in 2003. They hired a manager from the fashion world, Wilson, to take the helm; He felt the traditional customer should be abandoned and a younger, hipper crowd captured. In 2006, with the choice of Sadove, they seem to desire emphasis upon classic style, luxury apparel and value for the traditional customer. He seems well positioned to navigate this course. The board ultimately chose Strategy 3. What was the decision in 2003 and did they made a tactical mistake in choosing Wilson? We do not know from the information. Given the information in CaseCo, Strategy 3 seems the natural choice. Strategy 1 was to move to the middle of the spectrum, which was not working for Saks at the time. We could say it was a move from Cadillac to a really nice Chevy. Was the base moving this way or was the base becoming more affluent? If Saks doesn't sell "snooty," what does it sell differently from the competition? Strategy 2 entailed abandoning the customer base instead of refocusing on the customer's desires. Strategy 2 held greater risk than Strategy 3 as one doesn't know how 30-something would react to a suped up Caddy with a BMW logo.

The SaLT Circle now appears concentric. Emphasize classic style, luxury apparel and value for the traditional customer. In terms of the SaLT Decision Tree, Saks lost its niche and is struggling to find it again through alignment discussed in SaLT Step Figure 4.1. We will have to wait and see the outcome.

Sources: *Neiman Marcus, Nordstrom and Saks Websites*, *BusinessWeek*, "Saks Fights off the Ravages of Age" by Brian Grow and Dean Foust, 9 September, 2002. *The New York Times*, "Officials Say Saks Has Picked Its Next Chief" by Tracie Rozhon, 15 November, 2003, and *The New York Times*, "Saks Fifth Avenue Takes a Step Back in Search of Its Future", by Michael Barbaro, 1 June, 2006.

NOTES

1   *Chicago Manual of Style*, 644.

2   Eisenach and Miller, "Reaganomics."

3   Ibid.

4   National Archives and Records Administration, link: The Reagan Presidency.

5   Encyclopedia Britannica, article: classical economics.

6   Smith, *Wealth of Nations*, 23-24.

7   Encyclopedia Britannica, article: Adam Smith.

8   Levensohn, "Rites of Passage," 6.

9   Ibid., 8-9.

10 Johnson, "State of the Union Address, 1966."

11 Dallek, *Flawed Giant*, 300.

12 Ibid., 302.

13 Encyclopedia Britannica, article: David Ricardo.

14 Ricardo, *Principles of Political Economy*, chapter 7, paragraph 16.

15 Encyclopedia Britannica, article: Lionel Robbins.

16 Ibid., article: Thomas Robert Malthus.

17 Oxford, malthusian defined.

18 Malthus, *An Essay*, Book 1, Chapter 14, paragraph 16.

19 Ibid., Book 4, Chapter 2, Paragraph 10.

20 Encyclopedia Britannica, article: money.

21 Furness, *Island of Stone Money*, 91-106.

22 Friedman, *Money Mischief*, 7.

23 Peele, *7 Tools*, 24.

24 Ibid., 26.

25 The Economist, "Economics A to Z", search: ceteris paribus.

26 Jump The Shark, Inc., entry: The Addams Family.

27 Lewisohn, "The Addams Family."

28   Mill, *Elements of Political Economy*, II, II, 6.

29   Encyclopedia Britannica, article: James Mill.

30   Smith, *Wealth of Nations*, 572.

31   United Nations, "Press release #735."

32   Encyclopedia Britannica, article: weather forecasting.

33   Ibid., article: complexity.

34   Liggett, "Frank's Place."

35   Junger, *The Perfect Storm*, 112.

36   The Gallup Organization, "Bush Approval, May 9, 2006."

37   Knight, *Risk, Uncertainty, and Profit*. Part I, Chapter I, paragraph 26.

38   Bank of International Settlements, searches: history, fact sheet, operational risk, bcbs86.

39   Holton, "Defining Risk," 24.

40   Amazon, entry: A Simple Plan.

41   Encyclopedia Britannica, article: oligopoly.

42   FindLaw, *Matsushita Electric Industrial Company v. Zenith Radio Corporation*.

43   Shepard, "Causes" 613-615, 626.

44   Princeton University, "Tucker Obituary."

45   ISCID, article: nash equilibrium.

46   Encyclopedia Britannica, article: John Forbes Nash Jr.

47   Allingham, *Choice Theory*, 78.

48   Nowak *et al.*, "Arithmetics," 76-81.

49   Leonhardt, "What Price Loyalty?"

50   Sperry & Hutchinson, link: company history.

51   Viacom, link: The Brady Bunch episode guide.

52   Associated Press, "Green Stamps Licked."

53   Aristotle, *Nicomachean Ethics*, Book VI, 2.

54   Encyclopedia Britannica, article: Edwards Deming.

55   Allingham, *Choice Theory*, 1.

56   The New School, search: subjective utility.

57   Encyclopedia Britannica, article: probability, search: Leonard Savage.

58   Encyclopedia Britannica, article: Blaise Pascal.

59   Pascal. *Pensées*, Section III, 233.

60   Encyclopedia Britannica, article: Blaise Pascal.

61   Ibid., articles: Thomas Bayes, bayes' theorem and bayesianism.

62   Bayes, "An Essay," Section I, Definition 5.

63   Thaler, *The Winner's Curse*, 68-70

64   Ibid., 64-68

65   Ibid., 70-72

66   Encyclopedia Britannica, article: Aesop.

67   Aesop, *The Hawk and the Nightingale*.

68   Ibid., *The Politicians*.

69   Encyclopedia Britannica, article: Vilfredo Pareto.

70   Konold, "Informal Concepts," 59.

71   Henderson, "Herbert Simon."

72   Simon, "Designing Organization," 40-41.

73   Encyclopedia Britannica, article: new madrid fault.

74   Anything Arkansas Directory, article: Crowley's ridge.

75   Waters, "Time."

76   Faulkner, *The Sound and The Fury*, 86.

77   Encyclopedia Britannica, article: John Maynard Keynes.

78   Keynes, "Keynes Quote #32508."

79   Caddo Lake, "History Page."

80   Bayus, "Product Lifetimes," 764.

81   Stern and Stalk, "Perspectives," 35-37.

82   Schnaars, *Marketing Strategy*, 39-40.

83   RMA, "Annual Statement Studies."

84   Seuss, *one fish two fish red fish blue fish*, title.

85   Malik, "Spacehab."

86   Encyclopedia Britannica, article: Ohno Taiichi.

87   Kahn and Egan, "Ain't we got fun?"

88   Horwitt, "Alinsky."

89   Lohr, "Growth Spurt."

90   Salesforce.com, homepage.

91   TurboTax, homepage.

92   PBS, "Alaskan Pipeline," link: Transcript.

93 Alyeska Pipeline Service Co., link: Facts.

94 ENR, "Construction's Man of the Year," 26.

95 Local 798, link: Homepage.

96 PBS, "Alaskan Pipeline," link: Transcript.

97 ENR, "Construction's Man of the Year," 25-26.

98 The Inflation Calculator, $1 in 1977 converted to year 2005.

99 Alyeska Pipeline Service Co., link: Facts.

100 Charles Schwab & Co., search: LUV, S&P 500, DJTI historical data.

101 Southwest Airlines, Co., link: About SWA.

102 Southwest Airlines, Co., link: History.

103 Simviation, link: 737 facts.

104 Fogg, "Headmaster Scene."

105 Schultz, "backstory."

106 Zebco, link: Spincast Products.

107 Rapala, link: Lures.

108 Salvation Army, "National Red Kettle."

109 NFL, "Vikings v. Cowboys 1998."

110 Palo Alto Software, Inc., link: Home.

111 Dostoevsky, *Bobok*.

112 Hemingway, *The Sun Also Rises*, 34.

113 Armstrong and Brodie, "Effects on Decision Making," 73-84

114 Ibid., 74

115 Ibid., 82

116 Ibid., 74

117 Charan, "Sharpening," 51-52.

118 Laurie, *et al.*, "Creating New Growth Platforms," 84.

119 Herzlinger, "Why innovation," 61.

120 Grichnik, *et al.*, "Manufacturing Myopia," 39.

121 TopLine Saddlery, search: westfield whip.

122 Zilco, link: about us.

123 Alighieri, *Inferno*, Canto II, 1-9.

124 Nichols, "Town Spotlight."

125 Project Community, "Vaporized—Part One."

[126] Fogerty, "Bad Moon Rising."

[127] Arkes and Ayton, "Sunk Costs," 600.

[128] Ibid., 591.

[129] Ibid., 595.

[130] Ibid., 599.

[131] Hunter, "Casey Jones."

[132] Lightfoot, "Sundown."

[133] Caldwell, "Can't You See."

[134] Altman, "Medicare and Medicaid," transcript.

[135] Successories, Inc., search: history.

[136] Ibid., search: change.

GLOSSARY

Boston Consulting Group (BCG) Model—Strategic decision model based on product life cycle.

BCG Model—See Boston Consulting Group Model

Ceteris Paribus—"All things being equal." An assumption economists use to simplify their models.

Classical Economics—According to *Britannica*, the English School of economic thought that originated in the late 18th century. Dominated by the work of Adam Smith and reached maturity in the works of David Ricardo and John Stuart Mill. It focuses on economic growth and freedom stressing free competition.

Corporate Culture—Personality of an organization. A bit of a misnomer as a corporation is a collection of people. Over time an organization can develop a form of personality in the way things are done; how it views the world; how employees are treated and how it reacts to internal and external forces.

Elasticity—Refers to the slope of the demand and supply curves, *ceteris paribus*, stable curves. The steeper the absolute slope the more inelastic the curve.

Endowment Effect—A decision bias where people place a higher value on objects they own relative to objects they do not.

Equilibrium of Supply and Demand—Where the curves intersect, all goods produced are consumed at a certain price.

Execution Risk—The risk of a plan going awry due to its complexity. Simple plans lead to lower execution risk. It is a function of the number of things that can go wrong.

Expected Utility—Choices are made among a given, fixed set of alternatives with known probability distributions of outcomes for each alternative in such a way as to maximize the expected value of a given utility function.

Fixed Costs—Costs that do not vary with output. They can be lumpy and vary at different levels or scale of output.

Invisible Hand—Integration of supply and demand that efficiently allocates goods in an economic system. From Adam Smith

Ivory Tower Effect—Tendency to isolate and lose perspective.

Law of Demand—"All things being equal" the higher a good's cost or price the less consumers will demand or consume it.

Law of Supply—Inverse of demand. The higher the price, the more of a good the supplier is willing to produce for sale.

Law of Diminishing Returns—When one of the factors of production is held fixed, increasing the other factors will lead to an increase in returns up to a point. Beyond this point returns will diminish.

Logistics—Having the right thing in the right place at the right time.

Loss Aversion—Decision bias where people strongly prefer avoiding losses than acquiring gains.

Monopoly—Exclusive control or possession in the trade of a product. Monopolies can be natural, or created by privilege or collusion. An example would be the local power company because of barriers to entry, although control has been hypothetically stripped by regulation.

Monopolistic—Characterized by many of the traits of a pure monopoly.

Malthusian Catastrophe—The idea that humanity's population growth would outstrip the ability feed itself. Thomas Robert Malthus was consumed with the idea.

Marginal Physical Product (MPP)—Change in output as input changes.

Money—A generally accepted medium of exchange.

MPP—See Marginal Physical Product.

Nash Equilibrium—A collective strategy in a game involving two or more players, where no player has anything to gain by changing only his or her own strategy.

Natural Size—Given the cost structure of a business and the lumpiness of fixed costs, a business may have an optimal size or sizes to maximize profitability.

Niche—A specialized product or service that gives you monopolistic market power.

Non-Price Competition—Product differentiation. Can take many forms such as branding, actual product differentiation and incentives.

Oligopoly—Limited competition between a small number of sellers.

Oligopolistic—Characterized by many traits of an oligopoly.

Opportunity Cost—What you give to get something else.

Pascal's Wager—An example of choice under uncertainty. If you must wager that God exists, wager that he does as winning holds infinite reward.

Price Discrimination—When a different price is charged to customers for the same product. For producers, the perfect world would be one in which they could charge each customer a different price; the price that each customer would be willing to pay.

Prisoner's Dilemma—In game theory, it depicts two partners in crime confronted with the following choices. If one confesses and the other does not, the confessor receives a short sentence and the other goes to jail for a long time. If neither confesses, each goes free. If both confess, each goes to jail for a short period of time. Each reasons that he is better off confessing.

Production Possibilities Curve (PPC)—Output of goods that an economic system can produce. Denoted by the production possibility frontier.

Product Life Cycle—Products and companies mimic biological life in that a product passes through birth, growth, maturity, decline and death.

Pure Competition—Classic form of competition in economic analysis with five tests. Rarely encountered in the real world.

PWS—The confluence of product, widget and service and the corresponding value given to your customer. Envisioned on a continuum.

Rationality—In economics and choice theory means acting in terms of one's desires. It does not consider if those desires are in and of themselves "rational."

Real World—Versus an academic, hypothetical or desirable world; Describes how things really function.

Risk—A chance or possibility of danger, loss, injury or other adverse consequence. A measurable uncertainty.

SaLT—The integration of an organization's strategy, logistics and tactics in order to achieve its goals over time.

Satisfice—To get a result that is good enough, but not the best. A term used in respect to bounded rationality.

SBO—The small business owner: usually the founder.

Scarcity—Resources are limited as compared to humanity's wants and desires.

Stagflation—An economic condition characterized by high inflation and low growth.

Status Quo Bias—In decision making, an option is more desirable because it is the status quo and for no other reason.

Strategy—A plan of action.

Subjective Utility—Because of limited information, we maximize utility on a subjective basis. Outcomes and the probabilities are subject to our beliefs.

Tactic—Poking the opponent in the eye when he/she hits you in the stomach. A device employed to carry out a plan.

Values—One's judgment of what is valuable or important in life.

Variable Costs—Costs that vary with output.

Volatility—A measure of risk that denotes variance of outcome.

Widget—A gadget or device.

BIBLIOGRAPHY

Aesop. *Aesop's Fables Online Edition.*
   http://www.pacificnet.net/~johnr/aesop/asearch.html (6 May 2006).

Alighieri, Dante. *The Divine Comedy:* Translated by James Finn Carter.
   Stony Brook, N.Y. Italian Studies at Stony Brook.
   http://www.italianstudies.org/comedy/Inferno3.htm (11 July 2006).

Allingham, Michael. *Choice Theory: A Very Short Introduction.* New York:
   Oxford University Press, 2002.

Altman, Ph.D., Drew. "Medicare and Medicaid at 40: A Retrospective."
   26 July 2005. *Kaisernetwork.org.* Kaiser Family Foundation.
   http://www.kaisernetwork.org/health_cast/uploaded_files
   /072605_kff_40th_transcript.pdf (22 July 2006).

Alyeska Pipeline Service Co. "Pipeline Facts." *Alyeska Pipeline.*
   http://www.alyeska-pipe.com/pipelinefacts.html (22 May 2006).

Amazon. *The Internet Movie Database (IMDb).*
   http://www.imdb.com/(11 May 2006).

Anything Arkansas Directory. "Crowley's Ridge." *Arkansas Encyclopedia.*
   http://www.anythingarkansas.com/arkapedia/pedia/
   Crowley's_Ridge/(11 July 2006).

Aristotle. *Nicomachean Ethics:* Translated by W.D. Ross. Evanston, Ill.
   Theology Website.
   http://www.theologywebsite.com/etext/aristotle/
   nicomachaen.shtml (17 May 2006).

Arkes, Hal R., and Peter Ayton. "The Sunk Cost and Concorde Effects:
   Are Humans Less Rational Than Lower Animals?" *Psychological
   Bulletin* 125, no. 5 (1999): 591-600.

Armstrong, J. Scott, and Roderick J. Brodie. "Effects of Portfolio Planning Methods on Decision Making: Experimental Results." *International Journal of Research in Marketing* 11 (1994): 73-84.

Associated Press. "Green Stamps licked: Final holdout gives up." *Portsmouth Herald (N.H.)*, 15 February 2003, http://www.seacoastonline.com/2003news/02152003/biz_nati /13098.htm (11 May 2006).

Bank of International Settlements. *Bank of International Settlements (BIS).* BIS. http://www.bis.org/about/index.htm (11 July 2006).

Bayes, Thomas. "An Essay Towards Solving the Problem in the Doctrine of Chances." *Philosophical Transactions.* 1763. http://www.stat.ucla.edu/history/essay.pdf (11 July 2006).

Bayus, Barry L. "An Analysis of Product Lifetimes in a Technologically Dynamic Industry." *Management Science* 44, no. 6 (1998): 763-75.

Caddo Lake. *Caddo Lake History Page.* http://www.caddolake.com/history.htm (11 June 2006).

Caldwell, Toy. "Can't You See." *The Marshall Tucker Band.* Capricorn Records, 1973.

Chicago Manual of Style edited by University of Chicago Press Staff. 15th ed. Chicago: The University of Chicago, 2003.

Charan, Ram. "Sharpening Your Business Acumen." *Strategy+Business* 42 (2006): 49-57.

Charles Schwab & Co. *Charles Schwab Member's Service.* fttp://www.schwab.com (11 July 2006).

Dostoevsky, Fyodor. *Bobok.* Dostoevsky Website, 1873. http://www.fyodordostoevsky.com/etexts/bobok.txt (11 July 2006).

Dallek, Robert. *Flawed Giant: Lyndon Johnson and His His Times 1961-1973.* New York: Oxford University Press, 1998.

Eisenach, Jeffry A., and James C. Miller III. "History and Culture: Reaganomics." *Hoover Digest* 4 (2004). http://www.hooverdigest.org/044/eisenach.html (6 May 2006).

Encyclopedia Britannica. *Encyclopedia Britannica Online, 2006.* Encyclopedia Britannica Premium Service. http://www.britannica.com (11 July 2006).

ENR. "Construction's Man of the Year: Frank P. Moolin, Jr." *Engineering News-Record*, 19 February 1976, 22-26.

Faulkner, William. *The Sound and The Fury*. New York: Vintage Books, 1987.

FindLaw, a Thomson Business. "United States Supreme Court Decision: Matsushita Electric Industrial Company v. Zenith Radio Corporation, 475 U.S. 574, 588 (1986)." *FindLaw*. http://caselaw.lp.findlaw.com/scripts/getcase.pl?court=US&vol=475&invol=574 (11 July 2006).

Fogerty, John. "Bad Moon Rising." *Creedence Clearwater Revival:_Green River*. Fantasy, 1969.

Fogg, Adam. "Monty Python's: The Meaning of Life Script." *Intriguing.com*. Adam Fogg. http://www.intriguing.com/mp/_scripts/meanlife.asp (11 July 2006).

Friedman, Milton. *Money Mischief: Episodes in Monetary History*. New York: Harcourt Brace Jovanovich, 1992.

Furness, W.H. *The Island of Stone Money: Uap of the Carolines*. Philadelphia: J.B. Lippencott CO, 1910.

Grichnik, Kaj, Conrad Winkler, and Peter von Hochberg. "Manufacturing Myopia." *Strategy+Business* 42 (2006): 37-47.

Hemingway, Ernest. *The Sun Also Rises*. New York: Charles Scribner's Sons, 1926.

Henderson, David R., editor. *The Concise Encyclopedia of Economics*. Liberty Fund. http://www.econlib.org/library/CEE.html (11 July 2006).

Herzlinger, Regina E. "Why Innovation in Health Care Is So Hard." *Harvard Business Review* 84, no. 5 (2006): 58-66.

Holton, Glyn A. "Defining Risk." *Financial Analysts Journal* 60, no. 6 (2004): 19-25.

Horwitt, Sanford D. "Alinsky: More Important Now Than Ever." *The Progress Report.* The Progress Report. http://www.progress.org/alinsky.htm (11 July 2006).

Hunter, Robert. "Casey Jones." *Grateful Dead: Workingman's Dead.* Warner Bros. Records, 1970.

Intuit Inc. *TurboTax.* http://turbotax.com (11 July 2006).

ISCID. *Encyclopedia.* International Society for Complexity, Information. http://www.iscid.org/encyclopedia/(30 June 2006).

Johnson, Lyndon B. "State of the Union Address, 1966." *The Presidents.* PBS: American Experience. http://www.pbs.org/wgbh/amex/presidents/36_l_johnson/psources/ps_union66.html (21 May 2006).

Jump the Shark, Inc. *Jump The Shark.* http://www.jumptheshark.com/(11 July 2006).

Junger, Sebastion. *The Perfect Storm: A True Story of Men Against the Sea.* New York: W.W. Norton & Company, 1997.

Kahn, Gus, and Raymond B. Egan. "Ain't We Got Fun." *341st Bomb Group.* 341st Bomb Group. http://www.341stbombgroup.org/music/aint-we-got-fun.htm (11 July 2006).

Keynes, John M. "Keynes Quote #32508." *The Columbia World of Quotations.* Bartleby.com. http://www.bartleby.com/66/8/32508.html (11 July 2006).

Knight, Frank H. *Risk, Uncertainty, and Profit.* Boston: Hart, Schaffner & Marx; Houghton Mifflin Company, 1921. http://econlib.org/library/knight/knrup1.html (11 June 2006).

Konold, Clifford. "Informal Concepts of Probability." *Cognition and Instruction* 6, no. 1 (1989): 59-98.

Laurie, Donald L., Yves L. Doz, and Claude P. Sheer. "Creating New Growth Platforms." *Harvard Business Review* 84, no. 5 (2006): 80-90.

Leonhardt, David. "What Price Loyalty? Something Free." *The New York Times*, 26 April 2006.

Levensohn, Pascal N. "Rites of Passage: Transition in Venture-Backed Technology Companies." *Levensohn Venture Capital Website*. Levensohn Venture Partners. http://levp.com/new/documents/riteofpassage.pdf (9 May 2006).

Lewisohn, Mark. "The Addams Family." *BBC.co.uk Comedy Guide*. BBC Worldwide. http://www.bbc.co.uk/comedy/guide/articles/a/addamsfamilythe_7770115.shtml (11 July 2006).

Liggett, Lucy. *The Museum of Broadcast Communication*. Museum of Broadcast Communication. http://www.museum.tv/archives/etv/F/htmlF/franksplace/franksplace.htm (11 July 2006).

Lightfoot, Gordon. "Sundown." *Sundown*. Reprise, 1974.

Local 798. *Local 798 Pipeliners Union*. https://www.local798.org/default.asp (11 July 2006).

Lohr, Steve. "Growth Spurt; A Cyberfueled Growth Spurt." *The New York Times*, 21 February 2006.

Malik, Tariq. "Spacehab Aims High with Apex Spacecraft Trio." *Space.com*. Space.com. http://www.space.com/businesstechnology/050824_spacehab_apex.html (29 May 2006).

Malthus, Thomas R. *An Essay on the Principle of Population*. 6th ed. London: John Murray, 1826. http://econlib.org/library/malthus/malplong6.html (11 July 2006).

Mill, James. *Elements of Political Economy*. 3rd ed. London: Henry G. Bohn, 1844. http://econlib.org//library/milljames/mljelm2.html (11 July 2006).

National Archives and Records Administration. "The Reagan Presidency." *Ronald Reagan Presidential Library*. http://www.reagan.utexas.edu/archives/reference/reference.html (28 June 2006).

NFL. "Thanksgiving Day Games." *Pro Football Hall of Fame*. http://www.profootballhof.com/history/stats/thanksgiving.jsp#90s (11 July 2006).

Nichols, Lynn. "Town Spotlight: Westfield." *Valley Viewpoint, 23 May 2002*. http://www.valleyviewpoint.com/spotlights/westfield.htm (11 July 2006).

Nowak, Martin A., Robert M. May, and Karl Sigmund. "The Arithmetics of Mutual Help." *Scientific American*, June 1995, 76-81.

Palo Alto Software, Inc. *Business Plans*. http://www.bplans.com/(11 July 2006).

Pascal, Blaise. *Pensées:* Translated by W.F. Trotter. 1670. http://oregonstate.edu/instruct/phl302/texts/pascal/pensees-contents.html (11 July 2006).

PBS. "Alaskan Pipeline." *American Experience*. http://www.pbs.org/wgbh/amex/pipeline/(11 July 2006).

Peele, Stanton. *7 Tools to Beat Addiction*. New York: Three Rivers Press, 2004.

Princeton University. "Obituary of Albert William Tucker, 26 January 1995." *Princeton University*. http://www.princeton.edu/pr/news/95/q1/0126tucker.html (11 July 2006).

Project Community. "Vaporized—Part One." *Pure Schmaltz*. http://www.projectcommunity.com/PureSchmaltz/files/archive-0.html (25 May 2006).

Rapala VMC Corporation. *Rapala Lures.*
http://www.rapala.com/products/lures.cfm?navoption=all
(11 July 2006).

Ricardo, David. *On the Principles of Political Economy and Taxation.* 3rd ed.
London: John Murray, 1821.
http://econlib.org/library/ricardo/ricp2a.html (11 July 2006).

RMA. "Annual Statement Studies." *Risk Management Association.*
http://www.rmahq.com/RMA/RMAUniverse/ProductsandServices
/RMABookstore/StatementStudies/(11 July 2006).

Salvation Army. "National Red Kettle Kickoff." *The Salvation Army of
Greater Dallas.*
http://www.salvationarmydallas.org/cowboys_kickoff.asp
(11 July 2006).

Salesforce.com, Inc. *Salesforce.com.* http://salesforce.com (11 July 2006).

Schnaars, Steven P. *Marketing Strategy: A Customer-Driven Approach.* New
York: The Free Press, 1991.

Schultz, Ken. "The backstory of the world-record bass." *ESPN Outdoors.*
ESPN.
http://espn.go.com/outdoors/tv/columns/schultz_ken/1988662.html
(11 July 2006).

Seuss, Dr. *One fish two fish red fish blue fish.* New York: Random House,
1960.

Shepard, William G. "Causes of Increased Competition in the U.S.
Economy, 1939-1980." *Review of Economics and Statistics* 64, no. 4
(1982): 613-26.

Simon, Herbert A. "Designing Organizations for an Information Rich
World." In *Computer, Communications and the Public Interest,* edited
by Martin Greenberger. Baltimore: The John Hopkins Press, 1971.

Simviation. "Simviation: Aircraft Information—737." *Simviation.*
http://www.simviation.com/rinfo737.htm (13 May 2006).

Smith, Adam. *The Wealth of Nations.* 5th ed. New York: Bantam Dell, 2003.

Southwest Airlines Co. *Southwest Airlines—About SWA.* http://www.southwest.com/about_swa/airborne.html (23 May 2006).

Southwest Airlines, Co. "History." *Southwest Airlines Media.* http://www.swamedia.com/swamedia/swa_history.html (23 May 2006).

Sperry & Hutchinson Company. *S & H Greenpoints Website.* http://www.shsolutions.com/(29 June 2006).

Stern, Carl W., and George Stalk, Jr. *Perspectives on Strategy from the Boston Consulting Group.* New York: John Wiley & Sons, 1998.

Successories, Inc. *Successories.* http://www.successories.com/(22 July 2006).

Thaler, Richard H. *The Winner's Curse: Paradoxes and Anomalies of Economic Life.* New York: The Free Press, 1992.

The Economist. "Economics A to Z." *The Economist.com.* http://www.economist.com/research/Economics/(11 May 2006).

The Gallup Organization. "Bush Approval Rating: May 9, 2006." *The Gallup Poll.* http://poll.gallup.com/(11 May 2006).

The New School, a University. *The History of Economic Thought Website.* http://cepa.newschool.edu/het/(11 July 2006).

The Inflation Calculator. http://www.westegg.com/inflation/(11 July 2006).

The Oxford American Dictionary and Language Guide. New York: The Oxford University Press, 1999.

TopLine Saddlery. *TopLine Saddlery: Products: Harness Racing.* http://www.toplinesaddlery.co.nz/products.php?cat=25 (11 July 2006).

United Nations. "Press Release #735." *The World Meteorological Organization.* http://www.wmo.ch/meteoworld/archive/en/october2005/recentevents.htm (11 July 2006).

Viacom. "Brady Bunch Episode Guide." *TV Land Website.* http://www.tvland.com/shows/brady_bunch/episodes/episodes1.jhtml (11 July 2006).

Waters, Roger. "Time." *Pink Floyd: Dark Side of the Moon.* Capitol, 1973.

Zebco. *Zebco Spincast Products.*
　　　http://www.zebco.com/catalog/spincast.html (11 May 2006).

Zilco. *Zilco: About us.* http://www.zilco.com.au/aboutus.shtm (29 June 2006).

INDEX
EXCLUDING GLOSSARY

978-0-595-42314-9
0-595-42314-0